IN FOCUS

JAMAICA

A Guide to the People, Politics and Culture

Peter Mason

LATIN AMERICA BUREAU

INTERLINK BOOKS
NEW YORK

© 2000 Peter Mason.   All rights reserved.
First published in 2000

In the U.S.:

Interlink Books
An imprint of Interlink Publishing Group, Inc.
99 Seventh Avenue, Brooklyn, New York 11215 and
46 Crosby Street, Northampton, Massachusetts 01060
ww.interlinkbooks.com

Library of Congress Cataloging-in-Publication Data

Mason, Peter, 1963-
    Jamaica in focus: a guide to the people, politics and culture / by
    Peter Mason.
        p. cm. -- (In focus)
    Includes bibliographical references.
    ISBN: 1-56656- 285-6 (pbk)
     1. Jamaica I. Title II. In focus

    F1868 .M37 1999   99-050202
    972.92--dc21

In the U.K.:

Latin America Bureau (Research and Action) Ltd,
1 Amwell Street, London EC1R 1UL

The Latin America Bureau is an independent research and publishing
organization. It works to broaden public understanding of issues of
human rights and social and economic justice in Latin America and the
Caribbean.

A CIP catalogue record for this book is available from the British
Library
ISBN: 1 899365 40 0

Editing: Jean McNeil
Cover photograph: Ian Cumming
Cover design: Andy Dark
Design: Liz Morrell
Cartography and diagrams: Catherine Pyke

Already published in the *In Focus* series:
Argentina, Bolivia, Brazil, Chile, Colombia, Costa Rica, Cuba,
Dominican Republic, Eastern Caribbean, Ecuador, Guatemala, Jamaica,
Mexico, Nicaragua, Peru, Venezuela

Printed and bound in Korea

CONTENTS

Introduction: The Best and the Worst   4

1 ——— Land and People: From Mountains to Ghettos 6
Kingston
Spanish Town
"Out of many..."

2 ——— History: Island of Conflict 13
Columbus and After
Pirate Capital
"King Sugar"
The Road to Independence

3 ——— Politics: Violent Democracy 30
"Better Must Come"
"Deliverance"
The PNP Returns

4 ——— Society: Hard Times 36
Health Services
Women and Families
Crime
Rastafarianism

5 ——— Economy: Elusive Riches 51
Bauxite
Agriculture
Tourism
The Environment

6 ——— Culture: On the World Stage 63
Reggae
Art and Literature
Sport
Food

Where to Go, What to See 80
Tips for Travelers 85
Addresses and Contacts 87
Further Reading and Bookstores 88
Facts and Figures 90

INTRODUCTION: THE BEST AND THE WORST

Jamaica, like many Caribbean islands, is a territory of conflicting images. The positive ones are many: it can play up to its billing as a friendly, tropical paradise with as much aplomb as any of the smaller West Indian islands it competes with on the tourist circuit; it is a vibrant and innovative home to musical and sporting achievement, and it is a proudly independent, democratic society in a region where political stability is at a premium. It has natural riches and a lush beauty that are the envy of other Caribbean nations.

Yet the negatives are many, too, for Jamaica has a dark side that clouds its otherwise sunny disposition. It is a land where tens of thousands live in desperate poverty and unemployment, where the state struggles endlessly with debt and corruption, and where the economy forever seems on the verge of crisis. Jam is usually on tomorrow's menu, rarely today's.

Crucially, it is also a gun-ridden society where inequality, the drug trade, domestic disputes, political feuding, and gang warfare contribute to one of the worst murder rates in the world. Even the weather, idyllic for the most part, becomes a killer in the hurricane season. Life comes cheap, as it does in many other third-world countries.

Jamaica is a land of cheek-by-jowl paradoxes. Rich and poor are frequently separated only by a security fence, while the walls of the all-inclusive tourist resorts provide shade for makeshift villages of corrugated iron and cardboard. Behind the ready smiles of so many Jamaicans lies anger and resignation in equal measure.

Jamaicans are a proud and defiant people who will fight for themselves with ferocity, but who have also, through years of bitter experience, come to adopt a studied air of indifference on the grounds that it is better not to expect anything that is unlikely to be delivered. At times, in a land of great religious conviction where most draw hope from the bible, the country seems to be consumed with portentous gloom.

Jamaica, then, is the best of the Caribbean and the worst of the Caribbean, a country of highs and lows where the populace is often forced to ride a roller coaster of hope and despair. Whether the positive images outweigh the negatives is a matter for debate, but it is safe to say that most outsiders (as well as many Jamaicans) find it difficult to make up their minds. In any case, Jamaica is increasingly being defined as much by the activities

The residents of Cousins Cove, Jamaica   *Ian Cumming*

of its diaspora in the US, Canada, and the United Kingdom as by those who actually live on the island.

Positive or negative, Jamaica certainly makes a much bigger impression on the world's consciousness than it has any right to – and therein lies one of its greatest attractions. Whether you love it or hate it, it is difficult to ignore Jamaica's feisty presence.

This guide aims to examine that presence and to look at the historical and economic factors that have shaped it. It also aims to identify the rich cultural heritage that keeps the Jamaican people going in the face of such adversity.

1   LAND AND PEOPLE: FROM MOUNTAINS TO GHETTOS

The original inhabitants of Jamaica, the Tainos or Arawaks, referred to their territory as Xaymaca or "land of wood and water." There is less of either commodity these days – deforestation in recent years appears to have affected the island's micro-climate – but Jamaica is still a lush green island with 120 rivers, impressive waterfalls, huge amounts of rainfall in parts, and just under 25 percent of the land under forest.

The largest of the English-speaking Caribbean islands and second only in size to nearby Cuba and Hispaniola, it sits in the center of the Caribbean Sea as part of the Greater Antilles chain, more or less equidistant from the land masses of North America, Central America and South America. At just under 11,000 square kilometers (4,410 sq miles), it is slightly smaller than Northern Ireland, though significantly more crowded and with a population of 2.6 million growing at just under one percent per year.

Jamaica is a land not just of wood and water, but of spectacular hills. The cool Blue Mountains rise to 7,402 feet in the east, providing ideal conditions for coffee growing, while the bumpy and cave-ridden limestone "cockpit country" of the northwest, 2,400 feet at its highest point, is still remote and relatively inaccessible. Almost half of the country is higher than 1,000 feet above sea level.

Most of the north of the island is hilly country, spotted with villages and "provision grounds" where small landowners tend bananas, yams, sweet potatoes, and other staples. The only consistently flat area is the swampy region in the southwest around the small town of Black River, yet even here the Santa Cruz Mountains intervene. The nature of the landscape means that traveling around is not always straightforward, and though the island is only 145 miles (240km) from east to west and about 50 miles (80km) from north to south, a journey from one end to the other can, given the state of the roads and some of the terrain, take at least six or seven hours by car.

Although primary rainforest is now hard to find, Jamaica is, for the most part, as verdant as one would expect of a tropical island with average rainfall of 78 inches a year (198cm) and mean temperatures of 82F (27C). In the rain shadow of the Blue Mountains, however, the dry and largely uninhabited Hellshire Hills to the west of Kingston have a desert-like quality, with scrubby vegetation, iguanas, strange cacti, and sandy terrain bordering the sea.

Main beach in Ocho Rios   *Ian Cumming*

There are beautiful sandy beaches all around the island, but the north coast from Ocho Rios to Montego Bay generally has the best and – along with Negril on the western tip of the island – has become the main tourist area as a consequence. Except for Negril, where the beach runs uninterrupted for seven miles, there are few vast expanses of sand, with most beaches confined to sheltered bays and occasionally protected by coral reefs. There is cliff landscape too, notably the spectacular 1,500ft cliff at Lovers' Leap in the south, and tiny, scattered islands off Kingston. Everywhere along the coast self-employed fishermen ply their trade on the usually benign Caribbean Sea.

The island's natural resources are impressive. The soil is generally fertile and there are few areas of the country that cannot be put to some good use, with about 45 percent of the land under agriculture. Some of the large sugar plantations remain, and there are banana estates too, particularly in the northeast toward Port Antonio.

In the lower lying areas of the west, cattle farming is more common, and in the central region lie huge deposits of bauxite that have allowed Jamaica to become one of the world's largest producers of the ore used to make aluminum.

The biological diversity is stunning, with 320 species of hummingbirds alone and 3,000 flowering plants, many of them unique to Jamaica. Although the imported mongoose has wiped out many snakes, crocodiles can still be found in the Black River Morass and the island is rich in fauna and flora of all types. What nature gives with one hand, however, can be taken away with the other, for Jamaica lies in the hurricane belt and has been flattened on various occasions by a series of devastating storms, including Hurricane Gilbert in 1988. In a 100-year period, the island can expect to be hit by between 50 and 70 hurricanes of varying ferocity, usually between the months of July and November. Earthquakes are also a fairly regular feature; one of the worst, in 1907, destroyed large areas of Kingston.

There are environmental worries, too, mainly linked to rural poverty and land scarcity. Two-thirds of the poor live in the countryside, and badly managed subsistence hillside farming has created soil erosion. As population pressures increase, internal migration from rural areas to the towns has led to squatting on precious virgin land and further environmental damage. More than 55 percent of the population is now urbanized, and that figure is growing by two percent a year as more people drift into urban areas.

Kingston

Jamaica's capital lies in a majestic setting, dominated to the north and east by the Blue Mountains (so called because of the blue haze they take on from a distance) and defined to the south by the huge sweep of the seventh largest natural harbor in the world.

The city began to emerge in the 1700s, becoming the capital in 1872 when the British decided that its rapid growth and the importance of its port facilities meant it should supersede the former capital, Spanish Town. Now it is the largest English-speaking city in the Caribbean.

Kingston's climate is hot and mostly pleasant, but it can be airless at times, sweating in the largely breezeless shelter of the Blue Mountains. Then it is easy to feel the tension that, despite the idyllic setting, pervades an urban environment made angry by poverty and inequality. Kingston is a city on the edge, as periodic riots, disturbances, and gun battles testify.

Many sections of the capital, mainly the "downtown" and inner western areas nearer the harbor front, are replete with dread connotations, virtual no-go areas for those who do not live there. Trench Town is infamous the world over, thanks to the songs of Bob Marley, but names like Jones Town, Denham Town and Rae Town are also shot through locally with the fear that is part and parcel of ghetto life – as are particular streets, such as Lincoln Avenue, Greenwich Street and Grants Pen Road, which habitually feature as flash points in gun battles with police. In these crowded, semi-autonomous areas life can be short and brutal (especially for young men) as the daily hustle for a living inevitably works itself into the sphere of crime and drugs.

Communal tap, South Side, Kingston   *Marc French/Panos Pictures*

The violence and deprivation is not confined to these downtown areas, though, as the overspill residents of Riverton on the city's western edge or August Town on its western extreme would testify. Although some "uptown" parts of the city are disarmingly suburban, even they are rarely far from a squatted piece of land or a makeshift community built next to one of the huge storm gullies that criss-cross the city. And being in a "respectable" part of town only makes residents a target for armed break-ins: most Kingstonians are protected by security fences and guard dogs, but can usually still tell a personal tale of robbery or even murder that has directly affected them. Frequently they go to bed at night hearing the distant sound of gunshots.

It is easy to overplay the violence. Kingston may be an intimidating place, but it is no Johannesburg. To some extent, the danger is confined to those living on the front line, and casual incidents involving innocent third parties are uncommon on the main thoroughfares. And although ghetto life is tough, it also breeds a strong, exuberant sense of community that remains tangible in Kingston where it may have faded out elsewhere.

Despite its increasing sprawl and a population getting on for 800,000, it has also managed to avoid the worst excesses of big city madness. There are areas, with their pockets of gallery-fronted gingerbread houses, that retain some of the Caribbean charm of the old Kingston, and the huge Coronation Market brings a country feel to the center as hundreds of vendors travel in from rural areas to sell their fruit and vegetables.

Luxury villas for visitors on the north coast   *John Gilmore*

At its best Kingston is a vibrant, sensuous city of noise, chaos and bustle, with sound systems blaring out from bars, goats grazing the grass verges, street vendors blocking the pavements and passengers hanging off overcrowded buses. In general, the uptown north of the city (much of it technically not Kingston at all) is the most salubrious district, especially as it moves up into the foothills of the Blue Mountains in areas of conspicuous wealth such as Constant Spring and Barbican Heights, served by shopping malls with fast food restaurants and cinema complexes.

In the pleasant western suburb of Mona is the University of the West Indies campus, the neglected botanical gardens, the University of Technology, and a well-manicured reservoir where rich people pay to jog around its perimeter while security guards look on.

The harbor front is largely given over to industrial or port facilities, a hospital, the infamous General Penitentiary and squatted areas. Across the bay is Port Royal, notorious in the seventeenth century as the wickedest pirate city in the world but now, thanks to an earthquake that dropped most of it into the sea, a quiet fishing village on a spectacular spit of land known as the Palisadoes. The same spit houses the Norman Manley International Airport.

Not surprisingly, given its reputation, tourists rarely venture into the capital, except on air-conditioned coach trips to see the Bob Marley museum or to eat ice cream on the grounds of Devon House, a tastefully refurbished colonial-style mansion. The expensive high-rise hotels among the office blocks of the new Kingston business district are used mainly by visiting business people and airline personnel.

Spanish Town

The Jamaican authorities like to push the bright, bustling community of Montego Bay as the country's second city, and there is plenty of justification for their stance; it has an international airport and has grown significantly to a population of more than 60,000, thanks to its central role in the tourist trade. But in terms of history, the unloved city of Spanish Town (50,000), just a short distance to the west of Kingston has better claim to the title.

In some ways Spanish Town is rougher and even more desperate than Kingston, having fallen victim to all of the capital's social problems, yet able to boast few of its saving graces. The center of the city is ramshackle and threatening, and little remains architecturally of its colonial past. A sign on its outskirts proclaims the fact that it was the nation's capital for more than 300 years, yet only its name and a residual role as the administrative center for birth certificates reminds the nation that this was once the hub of Spanish-ruled Jamaica.

If anything, the Spanish Town slums are worse than in Kingston, and the levels of violence are certainly comparable. Even its main open space, the Prison Oval, is grim and uninviting. Worryingly for Kingstonians, the thirteen-mile gap between Spanish Town and the capital, already partially filled in by the depressing new town of Portmore, is lessening by the year, so that the whole area could soon become one huge conurbation.

Far more appealing is Mandeville, in the central south part of the island, which is known for its cooler climate and was once used by the British as a hill station. Now it is favored as a settling down point for Jamaicans coming back to retire from emigrant exile in the US, Canada and the UK, and its population is expanding accordingly.

Despite the increasing urbanization of Jamaica, it still clings hard to its rural roots. The island is divided into the three counties of Cornwall, Middlesex and Surrey, which have little relevance to anyone, but the thirteen rural parishes they contain have much greater significance, and many Jamaicans will identify themselves by the parish they hail from rather than the obscure village in which they were born. When "country come to town" in search of a new life, the names of each parish – St. James, Hanover, Trelawny, Westmoreland, St. Elizabeth, Manchester, Clarendon, St. Ann, St. Catherine, St. Mary, St. Andrew, St. Thomas, and Portland – take on a special resonance for the homesick.

"Out of many..."

Although the urban areas, particularly Kingston, are slightly more cosmopolitan than the rural regions, the majority of Jamaicans are the descendants of West African slaves brought over in the eighteenth century. A few – the Maroons, whose ancestors escaped slavery to set up independent villages in the remote areas of the cockpit country and the Blue Mountains – have been able to retain much more of their African heritage. But most Jamaicans, thanks to historical intermixing with whites, belong to a population that is many shades of black, and though racial discrimination is supposed to be a thing of the past, Jamaica still suffers from an ingrained "pigmentocracy" that values light skin above a brown complexion and brown skin above black.

Whites make up no more than four percent of the population, but they continue to play a disproportionate role in the business life of the country, as they have done, until recently, in its political affairs. Many whites are now of Lebanese descent (known locally as "Syrians") thanks to an influx of immigrants in the early 1900s. A tiny Germanic presence exists in the remote village of Seaford Town, where blond, hillbilly descendants of several German families still farm land given to their forebears in the 1830s as part of an unsuccessful settlement plan.

Although the motto at the base of the Jamaican national coat of arms reads "out of many one people," the racial mix in Jamaica is far less diverse than in many other Caribbean islands, with 91 percent of the population of Afro-Jamaican or mixed-race descent. Unlike other West Indian territories, such as Trinidad, Guyana, or Guadeloupe, only a small population of East Indian origin remains in Jamaica, descended from indentured laborers brought over to work on the sugar estates between 1845 and 1916. They make up about three percent of the population and are now largely integrated into the wider community, both rural and urban. An even smaller Chinese presence, also descended from indentured laborers and particularly successful in business, accounts for about 1.5 percent of the population.

The original inhabitants of Jamaica were wiped out in quick time by the Spanish colonists, and though native Indian blood may be in the population somewhere, the main Taino legacy is in the form of words – such as barbecue, hurricane, hammock, tobacco, and canoe – that have survived from their language. English may now be the official tongue of Jamaica, but the majority, of whatever race, speak a distinctive and lyrical patois that has evolved over many years and is claimed by some to be a "nation language" in its own right. However it is defined, it has become one of the key ingredients that binds together a society forged from a history of division and conflict.

2   HISTORY: ISLAND OF CONFLICT

Jamaica appears to have been untouched by humans until about 650 AD, when the first wave of Tainos arrived by canoe from other islands to the west.

A generally peaceful, seafaring people who lived mainly on the coastline and along rivers, the Tainos originated from the northern part of the South American mainland in what is now Venezuela, Guyana, Surinam, and French Guiana, and had ventured out in search of new territory. Arriving first in Trinidad, they worked their way up the Lesser Antilles to Puerto Rico and, rather late in the day, over to Jamaica, Haiti, and Cuba.

In later years they were followed by the Caribs, more warlike Amerindians who also hailed from South America and who re-colonized the Caribbean islands for themselves, usually supplanting the Tainos in the process. By the time the first Europeans visited Jamaica, however, the Tainos were still in place, for the Caribs had not yet reached the island.

Archaeological evidence, most notably at White Marl near Spanish Town, shows that the Arawaks lived in relatively large numbers all over Jamaica, in small thatched-hut villages presided over by chiefs or *caciques* who were permitted several wives. They relied heavily on seafood for sustenance, but also hunted birds and iguanas (with now-extinct barkless dogs called *alcos*), smoked tobacco and cultivated native crops such as cassava, maize, and sweet potato. Undisturbed by the Caribs, they lived a largely peaceful existence until the arrival of the Spanish.

Columbus and After

Christopher Columbus landed at Dry Harbour, now Discovery Bay, on the north coast of Jamaica on May 4, 1494. He had made his first voyage to the Caribbean two years earlier and was now on a follow-up trip, looking for what he believed was "the Indies," a land of gold and untold riches.

Initial resistance from the Tainos in Jamaica was put down brutally with guns and dogs, after which the indigenous inhabitants agreed to provide food and trade as Columbus and his crew continued sailing toward Montego Bay. Following a diversion to Cuba, they returned to sail around most of the island before disappearing to Hispaniola (the island now divided between Haiti and the Dominican Republic). Fulsome in his praise for its beauty, Columbus had christened his "discovery" Santiago, but the Taino name proved more popular and Jamaica it remained.

Nine years later, on his fourth journey to the New World, Columbus revisited the island in more straitened circumstances when his two battered ships, *Capitana* and *Santiago*, limped into St. Ann's Bay on June 23, 1503 before sinking a few hundred yards offshore. The crew settled down for a long period of hardship and sickness there, trading what they could with the Tainos while a canoe was sent to summon help in Hispaniola. It took a year for grudging aid to come, during which time increasingly desperate crew members began to mutiny and abuse their native hosts. When help finally arrived, the 100 survivors were shipped back to Spain, where Columbus died not long after.

These initial European contacts with the island had been stressful for the Tainos, but fleeting and manageable. What came after Columbus was to lead to their eradication.

Under Columbus's son, Diego, who administered Jamaica from Hispaniola until Juan de Esquival was appointed the first governor, Spain began to encourage settlement of the island from 1510 onward. Those few who were willing to decamp to such a dangerous backwater took a terrible toll on the Taino population, killing them for sport or literally working them to death as slaves in mines where no gold was ever found.

Those Tainos who did not die from overwork, under-nourishment or ill-treatment in the mines or the fields were forced to neglect the indigenous *conuco* system of agriculture that had used local resources efficiently without damaging soil fertility. Crops were trampled or eaten by imported cattle and pigs, and supplementary hunting, fishing, and gathering fell into decline as the male Amerindian labor force was moved elsewhere to meet Spanish priorities.

The diet of the Tainos suffered horribly, and many died as a result. It also made them more susceptible to imported diseases, such as smallpox, measles, or the common cold. As they became weaker and more subjugated, many chose suicide as a better way out. Within 25 years of the first fatal encounter at Discovery Bay, virtually the entire population of Tainos – maybe several hundred thousand – had been wiped out.

Spanish Backwater

Despite their unflinching use of unpaid indigenous labor, the small population of Spaniards could not make a success of life on the island. Although in 1534 they quickly decamped from the frontier town of Sevilla Nueva in St. Anns Bay to the more favorable surroundings of Villa de la Vega (now Spanish Town), and later introduced bananas and citrus fruits as well as sugar, cocoa, and tobacco, a combination of poor farming techniques, illness, lassitude, in-fighting, and ignorance ensured that prosperity was forever elusive. During most of the 300 years of Spanish rule under 20 governors, Jamaica was neglected by a mother country that was far more interested in the prospects of the American mainland and was content to use the island mainly as a supply point for re-stocking and re-fitting its ships. The colonists remained poor, backward and neglected, harassed by pirates and raided periodically by French and English vessels.

Long-standing English interest in the sparsely populated island finally crystallized under Oliver Cromwell in May 1655, when a fleet of 38 ships commanded by Admiral William Penn, smarting from a disastrous attempt to take Santo Domingo on Hispaniola, tried to salvage some pride by sailing to Jamaica. After landing at Passage Fort near what is now Kingston, Penn and 8,000 men were quickly able to engineer the surrender of the 1,500 Spanish inhabitants and burn the capital.

Pirate Capital

English settlers began to move to the island almost immediately, and by 1670, when Jamaica was officially ceded to England by the Treaty of Madrid after a decade of further skirmishes and guerrilla warfare, an expanding English community under a governor and a local assembly had been established. Most of the Spaniards fled to America or Cuba.

The English presence owed much in the early days to the activities of the Caribbean's buccaneers, a fearsome multinational crew of assorted desperadoes who were originally based in Hispaniola, where they lived in the wild parts hunting feral cattle and pigs. As the Spanish sought to bring them under control and deprive them of their livelihood, the buccaneers – mainly criminals and escaped indentured servants from England, Holland, and France – were forced to turn to more desperate survival techniques, chiefly piracy and pillage.

Bound together by a hatred of their Spanish persecutors, they formed a loose alliance as the "brethren of the coast," launching raiding parties to capture Spanish ships and sharing out the proceeds among themselves. Eventually they were openly courted by the English as a useful mercenary counter-force to the Spaniards, and began to base themselves in the burgeoning town of Port Royal in Kingston Harbor, where they could sell their loot, plot new ventures, spend their money, and while away their leisure time.

Port Royal flourished as a result, becoming a sordid regional flytrap for prostitution, slave trading, drinking, and gambling. For a short while in the late 1600s it earned a reputation as the richest and most debauched settlement in the New World, until on June 7, 1692 it was hit by a massive earthquake. The quake killed more than a quarter of the 8,000 inhabitants,

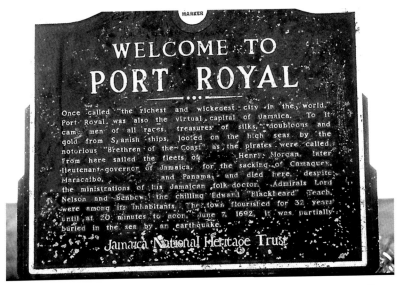

Port Royal, Jamaica

Howard J Davies/Panos Pictures

plunging half the town into the sea and forcing the port to be relocated across the harbor in Kingston. Many believed the disaster was divine retribution for Port Royal's wickedness.

One of the most effective buccaneer leaders of the era was Henry Morgan, the wild and ruthless son of a Welsh farmer. Morgan used Jamaica as a base for audacious, semi-sanctioned raids on Spanish towns in Panama and Venezuela. Eventually knighted, he settled down as a senior administrator and was given the job of trying to control the worst excesses of the sea rovers in Jamaica. Although he died at the age of 53 in 1688, he was able, as a merciless poacher turned gamekeeper, to persuade many of the buccaneers to take up farming or buy property and live off their ill-gotten gains. As a more stable era of civil government beckoned, the outlaws had lost some of their usefulness to the authorities.

Plantations and Slaves

The first half of the eighteenth century was a period of great growth for Jamaica as the new colonists (now officially "British" thanks to the 1706 Act of Union) shaped a plantation-based economy that began to reap real dividends for those who owned large tracts of land. There had been modest estates growing tobacco, cocoa, and small amounts of sugar under Spanish rule, but it was the British, less distracted by the lure of gold, who took agriculture further in Jamaica, introducing coffee in 1728 and moving the cultivation of sugar on to a new level.

The virgin soils of Jamaica were perfect for growing sugar cane, which had been imported to the Caribbean from Asia and had already proved to be a raging success for the British in Barbados. But cultivation was highly labor-intensive and it was only the growth of slavery that allowed the planters to make the estates work.

The Spanish had begun to bring in small numbers of African slaves within fifteen years of settling Jamaica, and as the Taino population dwindled, they drew more heavily on this source of labor. But it was the British, with their labor-hungry sugar estates, who upped the imports to much more significant levels.

Initially they had tried to encourage the use of white indentured laborers – mainly prisoners or debtors signed up on three to ten year contracts. But the supply of labor from Europe was short, the death rates were high, and the work rates poor. African slaves, by contrast, were cheap – especially after Britain's defeat of France in the War of the Spanish Succession, as the 1713 Treaty of Utrecht allowed Kingston to become the hub port for the slave trade. Transportation of the slaves formed one leg of a highly profitable three-stage journey from London to Africa, Africa to Kingston, and Kingston to London that kept ships full all the way. Goods for exchange with slave dealers went to Africa, slaves to Jamaica, and then Jamaican sugar for sale to London.

The number of Africans imported as slaves into Jamaica was huge: between 1700 and 1786 alone, 610,000 arrived at an average of 7,000 a year. By 1778, blacks outnumbered whites by eleven to one. Most had been sold to European traders working from slaving forts off the West African coast in the area now occupied by Ghana and Nigeria. They came from various different tribes, including the Yoruba, Fula, Ibo, Coromantee, and Mandingo, and were often sold by rival chiefs or Arab invaders who had captured them as prisoners of war. Others were simply snatched from their homes in the interior by raiding parties.

The human toll behind the trade was horrific, with the dreaded six-to-twelve week "middle passage" on filthy, crowded ships across the Atlantic incurring death rates of up to 30 percent. The survival rate was not much better once slaves arrived on the estates as field workers or domestics; about a third were expected to die within a year of arriving for sale in the Kingston slave markets. Those who survived were treated, according to the dispositions of each estate overseer, with varying degrees of brutality.

The Maroons

Not surprisingly, many of those who were dragged across the ocean did all they could to resist their plight, and from the beginning Jamaica had a strong tradition of slave rebellion. With its hilly terrain and large expanses of remote countryside, the island gave slaves a much better chance of permanent escape and survival than, say, the flatter and tamer landscape of Barbados.

The Spanish had set the foundations for this rebellious tradition by releasing (or losing control of) many of their slaves when the British arrived. Known as the Maroons (from the Spanish *cimarrón* for runaway), the majority settled down in the hills to live an alternative African lifestyle, punctuated by periodic battles with the British and raids on estates and settlements. Their village communities were supplemented at regular intervals by new waves of escapees – many of them Coromantees, who had a fierce reputation as spirited resistors.

The subject of the Maroons can be a touchy one in Jamaica, for while they are revered by many as heroic rebels, they are also criticized for what others regard as their treachery against fellow blacks. The main source of these allegations is the 1739 decision of the leeward Maroons of cockpit country, under chief Cudjoe, and the windward Maroons of the Blue Mountains, under chief Quao, to sign a peace treaty with the British. In return for full freedom and virtual autonomy, the Maroons agreed not only to put an end to their guerrilla warfare against the British but to return all newly escaped slaves to their masters. Nanny of the Maroons, a much celebrated female military leader who is now an official national hero, was unhappy with the agreement, but the Maroons subsequently played a key role in quelling a series of uprisings that helped the British maintain their ascendancy.

Those slaves who were left on the estates employed other forms of resistance, from violent armed struggle to poisoning, murder, theft, sabotage, the spreading of unsettling rumor, feigned stupidity, non-cooperation, strike action, spying, and riots. Regular uprisings were a feature of Jamaican life from the early 1700s onward, more than in any other British colony, and in 1760 a slave revolt led by a Coromantee slave named Tacky in the western parish of St. Mary's spread throughout most of the country. Though it was eventually put down, with the loss of 400 black and 60 white lives, "Tacky's rebellion" served as a blueprint for many other acts of rebellion.

Rebel slaves attack Montpelier Old Works, Jamaica, 1832

A Duperley

"King Sugar"

Despite the problems posed by rebellious slaves, many British estate owners grew obscenely rich on the new sugar-slavery system, which burgeoned from 50 sugar estates when the British arrived to about 430 by the 1740s and was now producing more sugar than all the other British colonies combined. The conspicuous wealth of the Jamaican whites became legendary in Britain, where the phrase "rich as a West Indian planter" entered the language and where, as absentee landlords who left their Jamaican affairs to estate overseers, many bought their way into high society.

The new riches bought power, too. Disputes between governors and the planter-dominated House of Assembly in Jamaica had plagued early British rule, but by 1729 the planters had become rich enough to pay the king £8,000 a year for guaranteed royal assent to the laws they passed. The deal handed Jamaican landowners significant autonomy, ensuring much smoother relations with the metropole for most of the next century.

The supremacy of "king sugar" continued throughout the 1700s, yet general turbulence generated by European political rivalries in the latter half of the century created some difficulties for the planters. A 1782 British naval victory against the French in the "Battle of the Saints" off Dominica and Guadeloupe stopped short a planned French invasion of Jamaica, but amid growing disgruntlement about the terms on which Jamaican sugar was exported to the mother country and worries about the early development of rival European sugar beet in the late 1700s, Jamaicans also had to contend with the disruption of the 1775 American War of Independence, which all but ended their trading links with America. Despite its riches, Jamaica was nowhere near self-sufficient in food, relying heavily on the Americans for staples such as salted cod. A British boycott on trade remained in place even after the war, and consequent food shortages in Jamaica led to the death by starvation of thousands of slaves.

A succession of devastating hurricanes in 1780, 1781, and 1784 compounded the problem by destroying crops grown by slaves on their provision grounds. The introduction of new plants such as ackees from West Africa in 1778 and mangoes from India in 1782 only partly ameliorated the problem, and breadfruit from Tahiti brought over by Captain Bligh had to be fed to pigs for many years before suspicious slaves would touch it. Diversification into coffee, cocoa, nutmeg, and cinnamon was more successful, but as the end of the century beckoned, the planters also began to face vocal calls for an end to the slavery system that had underpinned their riches.

Toward Emancipation

The fight to abolish slavery gathered pace in the mid-to-late-1700s, partly due to moral outrage in Britain inspired by the religious revivalism of John Wesley, the founder of Methodism, but also thanks to the humanitarian work of politicians such as William Wilberforce and Granville Sharp, as well as campaigning by some of the 10-20,000 people of African descent thought to have been living in Britain during the period.

After much maneuvering in the houses of parliament, where the planters had significant support, the British slave trade – though not slavery itself – was officially brought to an end by the Abolition Act on January 1, 1808. Denmark had already abolished its trade in slaves, but Britain was effectively on its own among other European powers and spent much time and money trying to enforce the new moral stance on its territories as well as the high seas.

Some Jamaican planters had actually supported abolition of the slave trade on the grounds that their slave communities were now self-generating, and that competitors who relied on imports of Africans to replenish their workforce would suffer as a result. But most fiercely opposed the next step of slave emancipation, arguing that without slavery the sugar industry would die. In this they had the support of some prominent members of the

Sam Sharpe

Anti-Slavery Society in London, including Wilberforce, who initially thought the idea of freedom for existing slaves was a step too far.

In many ways, the battle for emancipation was far tougher than the fight for abolition of the slave trade and it was here that the slave rebellions of Jamaica played a vitally important role in the struggle for slave emancipation in the British West Indies.

The long string of rebellions in Jamaica during the eighteenth century built up to a crescendo of slave uprisings in the period from 1800 onward, playing a key part in destabilizing the plantation system, terrifying the planters, and convincing Colonial Office administrators and British MPs that abolition would be a better option than the kind of slave revolution that had created the independent black republic of Haiti in 1804.

In Jamaica the most important uprising was the Sam Sharpe rebellion of Christmas 1831, when Sharpe, a slave and Baptist preacher, led a strike that developed into the burning of sugar estates around Montego Bay and many weeks of widespread rebellion over much of the island. After British troops restored order, the local landowners went on an orgy of revenge, killing and flogging suspected transgressors. Sharpe, now one of modern-day Jamaica's official national heroes, was hanged for his part in the disturbances.

The savage planter reprisals that followed such rebellions drew some sympathy and support for the slaves from the British public, and the Sharpe rebellion in particular acted as a catalyst for a renewed push for emancipation at a time of great unrest in London. The bill for damage and military costs caused by the disturbance was put at £1.25 million alone, adding to the already powerful economic incentives to get rid of slavery, which was increasingly being seen as an inefficient, as well as inhumane, way of doing business.

With cheaper European beet sugar now coming onto the market and the Jamaican sugar industry under pressure from more technologically advanced rivals in Cuba and Brazil, many British economists and free-traders, including Adam Smith, were inclined to see large, slave-reliant estates supported by sugar duties as an anachronism, especially when they were in uproar for much of the time.

Faced with the choice of emancipation from above or emancipation from below, British parliamentarians eventually chose the former. Two years after Sam Sharpe's rebellion – and after many years of planter-inspired prevarication – they passed an 1833 Emancipation Act that ended slavery in British territories from August 1, 1834 with the proviso that slaves would have to stay on their estates as part-paid "apprentices" for six years.

Full emancipation was finally achieved on August 1, 1838, when the much-abused apprenticeship system was scrapped and 311,070 slaves in Jamaica finally achieved their freedom. Jamaican planters were paid a total of £6.1 million by the British government in compensation – an average of almost £20 per slave.

Because land was relatively plentiful in Jamaica, many of the former slaves were able to abandon the hated plantations to squat or eventually buy small parcels of land where they could grow enough food to support their families and sell any surplus in the markets. Baptist missionaries encouraged the establishment of nearly 200 "free villages," such as Sligoville near Spanish Town, where people were able to create some sense of community after the alienation of slavery.

The Decline of Sugar

As the blacks drifted away from the plantations to a life of peasant subsistence, the sugar estates inevitably suffered. Already under pressure from foreign sugar rivals, suffering from reduced yields after more than 100 years of cultivation on the same soil, and riddled with inefficiency encouraged by complacent absentee landlords, they now faced a labor shortage.

In other areas of the Caribbean, the importation of indentured labor from India helped to prop up the sugar industry, but the notoriously stubborn Jamaican planters remained unconvinced of its value. Some Indians began to arrive on five-year contracts from 1845 onward, able once their contracts had expired to return home on an assisted passage or, after a ten-year period of residence, to stay on as free Jamaicans. Two-thirds chose to do so, settling all over the island and bringing rice cultivation to many parts, yet only 37,000 (plus 5,000 indentured Chinese) had come to Jamaica during the 76 years the indentureship system lasted, making little impact on the troubled plantation system.

Jamaica's post-emancipation sugar industry was propped up by British sugar duties that kept prices high and fended off foreign competition, but in 1846 even that protection disappeared as the British government, now firmly pro-free trade and industrialist in outlook, decided to use the

Equalisation of Sugar Duties Act to abolish duties protecting agriculture in the colonies.

In an alarmingly short time, sugar prices dropped through the floor, West Indian planter banks collapsed, and estates went to rack and ruin. Visitors to the island in the mid-1800s reported the complete collapse of the plantations as crops went untended, buildings crumbled, and tropical bush reclaimed the land. Almost as quickly as it had begun, the golden age of the Jamaican plantocracy was at an end.

The ex-slaves, now largely off the estates or ensconced in the towns, were partly insulated from the collapse, but many still relied on seasonal plantation work to supplement their incomes, and suffered accordingly. A population weakened by poverty succumbed to outbreaks of various diseases during the mid-century as 32,000 people died from cholera in 1850 and thousands more from smallpox in 1852. Later, the disruption to trade caused by the American Civil War (1861–1865) cut back supplies of grain and saltfish, pushing up food prices, which rose even higher during a severe two-year drought from 1863 to 1865.

Morant Bay

Life after slavery did not get much easier for the black population: they were still excluded from power, got the rough end of the justice system, often had high land rents to pay, and when there was work on the estates found the wages lower than ever. Emancipation had created a new set of economic and social tensions to succeed those of Jamaica's slavery era – and they soon culminated in the Morant Bay Rebellion of 1865.

The southeastern settlement of Morant Bay exploded on October 7, 1865, when Paul Bogle, political agitator and Baptist deacon, led a group of demonstrators to protest against the trial of one of his supporters. Scuffling broke out at the court and a warrant was issued for Bogle's arrest, but his supporters later fought off police attempting to carry out the order. Four days later, a reconstituted march, bigger than the first, re-entered Morant Bay and a riot erupted.

Dozens of demonstrators and police were killed as the disturbances spread through the area and planters were murdered in reprisals. Governor Edward Eyre, notorious for his harsh rule, imposed martial law before embarking on unprecedented retribution, executing 430 "rebels," flogging 600, and burning down 1,000 homes. Among those hanged were Bogle and his political ally William Gordon, one of a new generation of educated, largely mixed-race Jamaican agitators who had begun to push for radical reforms after being given limited voting rights in 1830.

Paul Bogle

The Morant Bay rebellion was essentially rooted in the failure of Jamaica's post-emancipation political economy. Emancipation had changed the social make-up of Jamaican society, heightening the expectations of ordinary people and switching their attention to the need for land and a decent income. Yet apart from the few "coloreds" (such as Gordon) who became small landholders, most people had little chance of bettering themselves, for Jamaica had moved into a prolonged state of economic and political decay. The Jamaican assembly largely did its own thing, for the most part ignoring Colonial Office officials by passing legislation that denied "free" ex-slaves the vote. Coloreds had a greater measure of political representation, but were still in a minority in the assembly and blacks were virtually ignored. In a system manipulated by the political authorities, magistrates sat in on cases involving themselves, made perverse rulings, and reinforced the racist social order.

General Eyre's murderous response to Morant Bay created the chance for change. The British government sacked him and imposed "crown colony government" directly from Westminster. With the planter-dominated house of assembly sidelined and waning in influence, significant reforms began to take place under new governor Sir John Peter Grant, who overhauled the police and judicial system, improved access to education, set up infrastructural improvements, moved the capital from Spanish Town to Kingston, and encouraged diversification into bananas, which began to fill the economic gap left by sugar. Although blacks were still excluded from most decision-making, a fragile peace reigned for much of the next 70 years as Jamaica tried to get back on its feet.

Raising the country out of its stagnation proved a difficult process, however, and though there were areas of improvement for an emerging black middle class, conditions remained poor for the vast majority of people. As the nineteenth century drew to a close, many Jamaicans opted for temporary or permanent migration to the north of the United States, to Panama to work as laborers on the Canal, or to the flourishing plantations in Cuba, Costa Rica, and Honduras.

Politics of Change

Political agitation during this period began to draw on the experiences of blacks – such as Dr. Robert Love and Marcus Garvey – who had experienced life abroad and had made contact with people of their own race in different settings. In 1906 Love won a seat on Jamaica's legislative council (formed in 1884 as a part-elected, part-nominated body to help crown colony administrators), but it was Garvey who was to have the greater lasting impact on black Jamaican consciousness.

Black Messiah

Marcus Mosiah Garvey, who was born in St. Ann's Bay in 1887, worked his way around South and Central America as a young man before spending time in England and, on his return to Jamaica in 1914, setting up the Universal Negro Improvement Association, dedicated to building an independent black state in Africa. The UNIA was a huge success, at its height boasting two million members in 40 countries across the world.

Under the banner "One Aim, One God, One Destiny," the charismatic Garvey traveled to New York in 1916 to rally American blacks with his Back to Africa message. He won many supporters and was able to start work on setting up the ill-fated Black Star Line steamship company, which aimed to help blacks relocate to Africa. Hassled by hostile US authorities, he was forced to return to Jamaica in 1927 after fraud allegations landed him in prison, and though he died in relative obscurity in London during 1940, his message still holds resonance for many Jamaicans.

Garvey's message did much to restore pride among the Jamaican majority, but it did little to change everyday conditions. When more than 10,000 Jamaican men came back from fighting in the First World War, they returned to the same old poverty, and when the Wall Street crash of 1929 plunged the world into recession, Jamaica was especially hard hit.

The Depression served only to emphasize the vulnerability of an island already blighted by habitually high levels of unemployment, under-employment and low wages. It also laid bare Jamaica's over-reliance on sugar and bananas, which were now being hit by disease and problems with soil erosion on overworked lands.

With work opportunities drastically reduced abroad, few Jamaicans were now able to look to emigration for work – and many of those who had left were forced to return to an island where the population was rising fast. Thousands drifted to the towns, where they fell victim to hunger, desperate housing conditions, disease, and crime.

Once again, Jamaica erupted in protest. Trade unions emerged after the Depression, and disturbances connected with worker organization generated into full-scale riots in 1938, when a strike for more pay at the West Indies Sugar Company's estate in Frome led to clashes with police, a handful of deaths, and serious trouble in other parts of the island. Alexander Bustamante, head of the Bustamante Industrial Trade Union, emerged as one of the chief protagonists.

Disturbances between 1935 and 1939 – replicated elsewhere in the British Caribbean – encouraged the growth, alongside the unions, of a new nationalist spirit that crystallized in 1938 with the formation, by Bustamante's cousin, Norman Manley, of the left-leaning Peoples National Party (PNP).

The PNP focused on the iniquities of British rule, which not only ignored the region's deprivations, but prevented the vast majority of Jamaicans from having a say in the way their lives were run. Middle-class blacks had dominated the toothless legislature since the 1920s and had entered the civil service and teaching profession, but only one in twelve of the population could vote under the crown colony system, which had rendered the local administration largely powerless. The new politicians put forward fresh goals of autonomy and eventual independence.

The response from the British was to set up a commission, under the chairmanship of the former Conservative MP Lord Moyne, to investigate conditions throughout the British West Indies. The Moyne Commission report, made public in 1945, recommended the setting up of a West Indian Welfare Fund to improve housing, health, and education, and called for the creation of labor departments, the introduction of land settlement schemes, and greater diversification in agriculture.

The Road to Independence

After the Second World War (during which Jamaica had proved a useful naval base and source of food), the British authorities set about trying to deliver some of these goals under a new constitution. Passed in 1944, it gave everyone over the age of 21 the vote and replaced crown colony government with a two-house legislature, under which one house was elected and the other was nominated. This was a significant step toward self-government – although under British rule and overseen by an executive council chaired by a governor. From now on there was no halting the gallop toward independence.

The first elections under the new system brought Norman Manley's PNP into power, with the newly-formed Jamaica Labour Party, under Bustamante's leadership, taking second place. The British, however, were beginning to push the idea of independence for Jamaica not on its own but as part of a united federation of the British West Indies colonies, with a regional parliament and constitution.

The idea was pulled into shape at a conference in Montego Bay in 1947, and by 1958, despite major misgivings in Jamaica, the ten-island federation (minus British Honduras and British Guiana) had formally come into existence.

Bustamante leads strikers in the 1930s

Serious inter-island squabbling – principally between Jamaica and Trinidad – hampered the federation from the very start as myriad issues, including import duty harmonization, economic policy, administration costs, and voting rights caused bitter disputes. In September 1961, when Manley held a referendum on whether to continue in membership, the Jamaican people voted for withdrawal. Trinidad & Tobago's Prime Minister Eric Williams famously declared that "one from ten leaves nought" and the federation fell apart.

While the smaller islands pondered their future, Jamaica was now ready for independence on its own – and the British were prepared to grant it virtually overnight. At a formal ceremony in the new National Stadium in Kingston on August 6, 1962 – less than a year after the referendum on federation – the union flag was lowered as the new black, gold, and green standard of an independent Jamaica was hoisted up.

The celebrations were joyful and long, but the post-colonial story has hardly ushered in much happier times for Jamaica. Although the black majority has at last got its hands on the reins of power, successive governments, now under the sway of the US rather than Britain, have unsuccessfully struggled to tackle the endemic poverty and violence that has been an intimate part of the island's history. Though Jamaica has remained a constitutional democracy, it has little to show, other than pride, for the struggles of recent years – and must, unfortunately, look forward to more pain in the twenty-first century.

3   POLITICS: VIOLENT DEMOCRACY

Jamaica's modern political life can be traced to the disturbances of the 1930s, when trade unionism and an emergent nationalist sentiment stirred the black majority to demand more control over every aspect of life. Although the likes of Marcus Garvey had raised the political consciousness of blacks in the earlier years of the twentieth century, it was the more conventional figures of Norman Manley and Alexander Bustamante who channeled this new awareness into concerted political action. Before their arrival on the national scene, Jamaica had no established political parties, only independents elected to a legislature that had limited decision-making powers under crown colony government.

Manley and Bustamante changed all that. Self-made, light-skinned cousins, the former a barrister and the latter a successful money-lender, they acted as the focus for worker discontent in the late 1930s and early 1940s, then negotiated Jamaica toward independence after the Second World War.

Both came to prominence as union leaders during the 1938 strikes and riots, when the charismatic Bustamante was jailed for seventeen months and the more assuming Manley fought for his release. While Bustamante took more interest in trade unionism, economic conditions, and the lot of the workers, Manley concentrated on calling for universal suffrage and an end to British rule, forming the social-democratic PNP in September 1938 as what he hoped would be a political adjunct to the Bustamante Industrial Trade Union (BITU) formed by his cousin.

Bustamante had other ideas, however. After his release from prison, he formed his own Jamaica Labour Party in 1943, and by 1944, when the first elections for a new House of Representatives were held, he ran successfully against Manley's party with a personal appeal to the working-class blacks who called him "the chief" and formed his main constituency.

The more left-leaning, intellectually inclined PNP quickly formed the Trade Union Congress (TUC) to counter Bustamante's BITU, and as tensions between the two factions turned into fatal workplace conflicts in 1947 and 1948, the violence that has marred modern Jamaican party politics began to gain a toehold.

Despite their trade unionist roots and working-class support, neither Manley nor Bustamante was a radical, and during the emerging Cold War period they spent much of their time trying to outdo each other in their condemnations of communism. Bustamante managed to steal a march on

Manley by vehemently opposing West Indian federation, but by the time independence dawned there was little to separate the PNP and the JLP other than the personalities of their two ageing leaders.

Elections in 1962 installed Bustamante as the first prime minister of an independent Jamaica with a parliament of two houses: the law-making House of Representatives, to which MPs from 60 constituencies are elected every five years, and the 21-member Senate, whose members are appointed by the governor-general, the prime minister, and the leader of the opposition.

Bustamante retired two years into his term, to be replaced by Donald Sangster, then Hugh Shearer, who won the next elections in 1967. Manley continued as leader of the opposition until shortly before his death in 1969 – "Busta" lived to be 93, dying in 1977. The main achievements of Bustamante and Manley – both now national heroes – lay in guiding Jamaica to independence, but it fell to others, chiefly Manley's son Michael and Shearer's successor Edward Seaga, to try to build something of the new Jamaica.

"Better Must Come"

Michael Manley, a union leader in his own right, swept the PNP to power for the first time with a large majority in the general election of 1972, ushering in a new era of more divisive, confrontational politics. He had quickly transformed the party he inherited from his father into a more youthful outfit, which promised an ambitious program of social and economic reforms and successfully appealed to the majority of the population who had been left out of a mini post-war economic boom built around the bauxite industry.

Under the party slogan "better must come," he advocated an essentially moderate course of action, but was not afraid to harness concepts put forward by the black power movement or Rastafarianism. During the 1972 election he carried a walking stick given to him by Haile Selassie which he dubbed the "rod of correction." He also promised the dispossessed "power for the people."

The pledges were easier to make than to achieve, however, and in 1974 a frustrated Manley announced his decision to take a far more radical, socialist tack that encompassed nationalization, land reform, increased taxation of the foreign companies involved in bauxite industry, and stronger links with the third world's non-aligned movement. The United States, frightened as always by the prospect of communism in its backyard, took an extremely dim view of Jamaica's new direction, especially its flirtations with Fidel Castro's Cuba, which began to lend a hand in various educational and health projects.

Manley's leftward lurch was mirrored by a rightward shift in the JLP where Edward Seaga, its Harvard-trained leader of Syrian descent, adopted an uncompromisingly right-wing stance that belied his party's union roots. With the effects of the oil crisis creating economic difficulties, aluminum companies scaling down their operations because of tax increases, and foreigners pulling out their investments in alarm at the government's "socialist" policies, the PNP's new strategy was hardly more successful than its original one. Although modest progress was made toward Manley's goal of promoting a more equal society – particularly through house-building programs, the introduction of a minimum wage, credit for small farmers, adult literacy initiatives, and free school lunches – the severe economic hardships and food shortages of the 1970s served to undermine most of what he achieved. Large numbers of Jamaicans, many of them wealthy and well-educated, emigrated to the US and Canada in search of a better life.

With Seaga railing against the "communist" PNP and the two parties dangerously polarized, the long run-up to the December 1976 elections saw political violence rise to new levels. Amid dark mutterings on the PNP side about deliberate destabilization and gun-running by the CIA, politicians from both camps armed their supporters in the Kingston ghettos, where the poor died in shoot-outs, bombings, arson attacks, and reprisal killings.

More than 100 people had lost their lives by June 1976 when Manley, to the dismay of human rights organizations, gave the police and the army special powers under an official state of emergency. The shootings continued on a smaller scale to the end of the campaign, in which Manley's democratic socialist platform still proved popular enough to win a 47-to-13-seat majority.

The PNP's second term of office proved just as difficult as its first. The continuing capital flight and financial crisis reached such catastrophic proportions that in 1977 and 1978 Manley felt he had no option but to take loans from the International Monetary Fund, the World Bank, and the European Community. The IMF terms proved ruinous to the PNP's social program, as public spending cuts were enforced and wage freezes took hold. Devaluation of the Jamaican dollar made imports more expensive and cut back food supplies, while the ghetto dweller, as usual, bore the brunt of the retrenchment. Walls in Kingston began to sport the slogan "the poor can't take no more," and in January 1980 Manley reneged on the IMF contract.

By October 1980, when Manley held early elections, the stage was set for another bloodbath of political gangsterism and upheaval in which an estimated 800 people were killed. Disillusion with Jamaica's plight was so great that the JLP was able to come to power with a massive majority on promises of a return to capitalism, market forces, and re-alignment with the US. But the savage election time conflict on the streets had plunged the country into further chaos and severely damaged its international reputation.

"Deliverance"

Seaga had promised "deliverance" to the Jamaican people, but he was as unable as Manley to get a grip on the debt-ridden economy. Some foreign capital reappeared, negotiations with the IMF were renewed, and large amounts of US aid were released by a thankful Ronald Reagan, who became Seaga's number one supporter. But the new money could not mask underlying financial problems, and as Seaga's government dismantled Manley's social programs and borrowed more, debts rose again.

The main political legacy of the JLP's rule was to bring Jamaica much closer to the US, which now embraced the island as a beacon of capitalist virtue in a rather suspect Caribbean Sea. The new relationship was epitomized not just by the dropping of diplomatic relations with Cuba, but by Jamaica's unstinting support for the invasion of Grenada in 1983, when Seaga sent in Jamaican troops as part of a US-led force to overthrow a Marxist coup.

In a move intended to capitalize on the popularity of the invasion in Jamaica, Seaga called snap elections two years before his term was due to expire. An outraged Manley, pointing out that updated electoral lists had not even been drawn up, boycotted the elections. The JLP won all 60 parliamentary seats, ushering in a period of one-party government that dented Jamaica's democratic credentials.

Always reluctant to delegate responsibility, Seaga used his unassailable position to take on a huge portfolio that added the finance and defense departments to his prime ministerial role. But his one-man show made little headway against poverty and unemployment, and in 1989, tired of IMF-inspired cutbacks and corruption, the electorate returned the PNP to power.

The PNP Returns

It was a chastened Manley who led the government this time, shorn of the 1970s socialist rhetoric, more concerned with building a political consensus and determined to portray a moderate pro-market image that would keep

Michael Manley

Marc French/Panos Pictures

the US on his side. Although he restored diplomatic relations with Cuba in 1990, he also toed the line with the IMF and established a dialogue with US President George Bush. In 1992 Manley resigned for health reasons (he died in 1997) and was succeeded by Percival (PJ) Patterson, an ex-lawyer, former manager of the legendary Jamaican ska band the Skatalites, and the country's first black premier.

Patterson, who committed himself to carrying on Manley's middle-of-the-road policies, continued to plot a business-friendly course after beating Seaga in the 1993 general election with a 47-seat majority. He was again returned to power in 1997 with a 50-to-10 seat majority as the JLP, still under the vice-like grip of a waning and unpopular Seaga, struggled for credibility.

Patterson's relaxed style of leadership has been low-key compared to the antics of his two predecessors, and some of the heat has been taken out of Jamaican politics as a result. The political scene is still potentially fiery, but has rid itself of the "big men" who have dominated it since the 1930s, and now has the potentially calming influence of a third party, the National Democratic Movement, which was formed in 1995 by ex-JLP MP Bruce Golding on an anti-corruption platform. Seaga stubbornly remains as JLP leader, but after years of polarization the two main parties have come closer together again.

Election time in Jamaica is always fraught, but the 1997 polls were relatively trouble free. A turning point of sorts came during the 1989 elections, when Manley and Seaga agreed to a peace pact aimed at reducing gunplay. The move was a success: although thirteen people lost their lives during that campaign and twelve died violently in the 1993 elections, the apocalyptic scenes of the 1970s and early 1980s have not been repeated.

Garrisons and Posses

Political violence is still an integral part of the Jamaican scene. Areas of Spanish Town and Kingston are divided into "garrisons" of JLP and PNP loyalty, where whole neighborhoods defend their turf and make sure the vote is brought in. Criminal gangs such as the JLP's notorious "shower posse" (so called because they shower victims with machine gun bullets) continue to make their presence felt, and although international monitors have pronounced themselves largely happy with the conduct of recent elections, corruption and intimidation of voters is an underlying problem. It is not unknown for vote counts in some wards to show 100 percent support for one of the two main parties.

The expected payback for garrison loyalty is favorable treatment in the form of employment offers, building contracts, and housing lets. Public works programs – such as the long-running development of the Coronation Market area in Kingston – are continually dogged by stop-go policies as one party begins a scheme in an area of traditional support, only to have it cut dead if it loses at the next poll. For many in Jamaica, politics is a matter of loyalty, identity, and patronage rather than ideology.

Now that the Manley era of third-world solidarity has passed, Jamaica's politics are far more aligned with the US and, on a secondary level, with the rest of the Caribbean. Friendly relations with the US are rewarded with increased trade opportunities, but the price is increasing interference in internal matters, especially over the drug war. Patterson has run into trouble for signing the controversial "Shiprider" agreement, under which US personnel can board boats in Jamaican waters to look for drugs.

More satisfying for those who want to preserve Jamaica's identity has been membership of Caricom, the Caribbean equivalent of the European Union. Caricom was moribund for many years after its creation in 1973, but has expanded to take in neighboring Haiti and now has increasing

Edward Seaga

Marc French/Panos Pictures

Roadblock, Tivoli Gardens, Kingston   *Marc French/Panos Pictures*

political influence in the region, especially in multilateral trade and aid negotiations.

The political links with Britain remain chiefly through the Commonwealth – of which Jamaica is a member – and the constitution, which gives the UK monarch a continuing, but marginal, role as the titular head of the country. There is widespread political support for making Jamaica a republic, a move that Prime Minister Patterson has promised to take forward.

The Jamaican love of debate about such issues is the salvation of its politics, for although the dark side of party activity has led to widespread cynicism and even hatred of politicians, it has not yet led to terminal apathy – as the frequent community actions and road blocks organized by local activists demonstrate. Ordinary Jamaican people still search passionately for political solutions, fired by the desperate need to eradicate poverty and unemployment.

36

4   SOCIETY: HARD TIMES

In terms of its performance in social indicators, Jamaica has some claims to being a middle-ranking country with respectable and improving scores in a number of areas. Average life expectancy, for instance, is a healthy 75 (compared with 77 in the UK and the US), and as regards mortality rates for under-fives, the island is level with Hungary, better than the Czech Republic. About 86 percent of the population has access to safe water, and more than 90 percent of children have been immunized.

The headline figures, however, mask a serious gap between the rich, who often live in great luxury, and the poor, whose access to the basics of life is severely restricted. About a third of Jamaicans live below the official poverty line – and to be below the poverty line in Jamaica is a serious business. The levels of squalor and deprivation of the slum communities along the roadsides of Kingston or in the rural interior match anything to be found in the rest of the third world. Unemployment is endemic, and a flimsy welfare system does little to ease the pain. Although there is a food coupon scheme for the most needy, one in ten children under five is moderately or severely underweight.

Despite the efforts of PNP administrations in the 1970s, little has been achieved at the governmental level to produce a more even distribution of wealth or to grapple with an essentially dysfunctional economy that makes life unstable for so many thousands of people. With state spending always under pressure and tax collection rates generally poor, there is little money in the welfare services pot to make life easier for the poor. Where government funds fail to patch up the holes, the emphasis is on self-help or a patchwork quilt of social services provided by the voluntary sector.

Health Services

Investment in the health service has leveled out to about seven percent of central government expenditure in recent years, about two percent less than in the 1970s and still below the defense budget. Most Jamaicans consequently find that medical facilities leave much to be desired, with long waits for treatment at the 24 general hospitals and 350 health centers, poor staffing levels, and under-funded facilities once they get to see a specialist. The wealthy use private services or fly to the US for more reliable treatment – as do many nurses and doctors in search of decent wages.

Inoculation has helped to improve public health, and since 1992 there have been no reported cases of polio, measles, or diphtheria, but AIDS has

Almond town, Kingston   *Marc French/Panos Pictures*

gone largely unchecked. An estimated 15,000 people were HIV-positive in June 1999, with four new people infected every day. Despite the input of the National AIDS Committee, costly treatment is available only to a few.

Housing

Health problems for many poor Jamaicans are exacerbated by appalling housing conditions, especially in squatted areas where whole families live in tiny shacks of wood and corrugated zinc. Squatting is the only way for many people to get a home or a plot of land, and has been on the increase in recent years. But successive governments, including those led by PJ Patterson, have promised "zero tolerance" for squatter communities, and have periodically sent in bulldozers to knock down fledgling townships. Meanwhile, much of the housing in Jamaica is truly awful, with conditions in rural areas just as bad as those in downtown Kingston. When a hurricane arrives, the homes of the poorest are often swept away.

The main source of finance for public house-building has been the National Housing Trust, which raises cash through a levy of two percent on each employee's salary, plus three percent of company wage bills. Most of the money is used to encourage home ownership, to carry out housing repairs, or to help land purchase. House-building programs have not always been a success; many medium-rise schemes in urban areas have quickly become as undesirable and crime-ridden as the run-down houses they replaced. A quarter of the population has no access to electricity or flush toilets.

Education

Schooling is free and compulsory only up to the age of eleven, although there is some state subsidy for education up to the age of fifteen. Because poverty forces many children to stay at home or work, education for the poorest section of society tends to stop at the primary level, with only two-thirds of boys and slightly more girls enrolling for secondary education. Truancy among those who have enrolled is also a continuing problem. It is not uncommon to see children begging at street corners, cleaning windscreens at traffic lights or helping their mothers peddle goods on the pavement.

For those whose parents can afford it, the best of Jamaica's secondary schooling is generally recognized to be of a good standard, with well-trained teachers who have long since moved away from the traditional Caribbean rote learning approach and who have achieved reasonable results given the crowded classrooms, poor availability of books, and dilapidated state of many school buildings. A selective system operates, but the old Common Entrance Exams for eleven-year-olds have been ditched in favor of a continual assessment process called the National Assessment Programme, which helps determine which school each pupil should go to.

This generally means, however, that the brightest pupils head for well-respected elite schools such as St. George's, Kingston College, and Campion, while the rest make do with what they can. Since 1975, when eighteen percent of government spending went toward education, government cutbacks have brought expenditures down to eleven percent, with a concomitant fall in standards. Two-thirds of those who take mathematics and English now fail their final secondary school exams.

At the higher education level, the main institution is the well-respected University of the West Indies, which has one of its three main campuses in Kingston (the other two are in Barbados and Trinidad & Tobago) and has provided many of the country's senior figures in public life. The more scientifically inclined University of Technology also offers degree level education and there are several teacher training colleges throughout the island.

Adult education is limited, and the adult literacy rate has been a long-term cause for concern. About 15 percent of adults cannot read or write, but that figure represents a considerable improvement since the early 1980s, when about a quarter were illiterate. The Jamaican Movement for the Advancement of Literacy (JAMAL) has helped deliver significant improvements in this area since its foundation in the 1970s.

Women and Families

Cohabitation and "serial monogamy" are more or less the norm in Jamaica and are certainly far more common than marriage; only one in ten Jamaican women is married by the age of 30, and many wait until their children are grown-up to put their "common law" relationships onto a more formal footing, if ever.

Coronation market   *Marc French/Panos Pictures*

Most women who have children do so with more than one partner, leading to flexible domestic situations where father figures may be absent altogether or for long periods of time. Although the average Jamaican woman now bears two or three children compared with five in 1960, more than three-quarters of babies are born outside of marriage. Young mothers are a widespread phenomenon: about 40 percent of Jamaican women are still in their teenage years when they have their first child.

As elsewhere in the Caribbean, the absence of a nuclear family structure often means that children are cared for by grandparents or relatives, or are brought up in extended families headed by older women. In general, "baby fathers" play a marginal role in child rearing, and many Jamaican children have to cope with a changing array of men in their family set-up.

Partly because of this, domestic violence and abuse within the home is a serious problem. Social and cultural traditions generally make life difficult for those who try to challenge violence against women, although the Domestic Violence Act of 1995 has helped by allowing restraining orders to be taken out against offenders. The incidence of rape is also alarmingly high (more than 1,000 a year) and, given the largely unsympathetic attitude within the police force, vastly under-reported. Sexual harassment in the workplace is also a problem: equal opportunities legislation dating back to the 1970s has had only a limited effect on discrimination, and some employers still expect sexual favors in return for job offers or promotion.

As in other Caribbean countries, however, Jamaican women have begun to carve out some improvements for themselves. About half are now economically active in the workforce (one of the highest rates in the world), and the hardships imposed by early motherhood or unstable relationships have made many Jamaican women strong, independent, and determined to improve their lot.

There have been breakthroughs in some areas, mainly those occupied by the middle classes. The majority of students at the University of the

West Indies campus are now female, and women hold about a third of senior civil service posts. Politics is also less male-dominated than before; Prime Minister PJ Patterson habitually featured two women ministers in his sixteen-strong cabinet during the late 1990s. But for most women, particularly the poor, life is a struggle against the odds for survival.

Emigration

With life so hard and job opportunities so limited at home, emigration has long been an escape door for many Jamaicans. An average of 22,500 people left the island each year during most of the 1990s, mainly, despite increasingly stringent immigration laws, for the US. Although emigration has helped slow down population growth to 0.9 percent a year and brings in valuable remittances sent to relatives back home, half of those who leave are between the ages of 20 and 50 – often the cream of the country's crop and sometimes some of the most skilled and qualified workers.

Although Jamaicans left for Panama, Honduras, Costa Rica, and Cuba in the early part of this century, modern-day Jamaican emigration effectively began with the fabled *Empire Windrush*, which sailed to the UK in 1948 with 492 Jamaicans on board as an advance guard of the new wave of post-war West Indian emigration. More than 163,000 Jamaicans settled in the UK between 1951 and 1962 as the labor-hungry "mother country" advertised in Jamaica for people to fill jobs in the Post Office, British Rail, London Transport, and the National Health Service. Increasingly tough immigration laws cut off the flow to a trickle by the early 1970s, when attention switched to the US and Canada. Since 1970, North America has attracted 85 percent of Jamaican immigrants.

An estimated 2.5 million "Jamaicans" now live all over the world, but mainly in New York, Baltimore, Boston, and Philadelphia in the US; London, Birmingham, Manchester, and Liverpool in the UK; and Toronto in Canada. Such a large diaspora has helped Jamaica exercise a cultural influence way beyond its size – and has fed back into the island itself, redefining the view of what it is to be Jamaican. Emigration to the US (much of it now illegal) has, in particular, contributed to the increasing Americanization of the island.

Returnees

An interesting flip side to the picture in recent years has been the arrival of "returnees" – Jamaicans who emigrated many years ago but have reached retirement age in their adopted country and now want to return to spend the rest of their days in the land of their birth. Since 1993 an estimated 20,000 people have picked up after a lifetime of hard work in New York,

Toronto, or London and settled in air-conditioned homes in the more salubrious parts of Kingston or in the quieter areas of the countryside, especially around Mandeville. Not all of them are retired.

The returnee experience has been a decidedly mixed one, as the attractions of Jamaica's climate, its sense of community, the slower pace of life, and the joy of coming home are counterbalanced by the difficulties of moving from the first world to the third. Many who have flown back from the gun-free, relatively peaceful environments of the UK and Canada have found the violent atmosphere of Jamaica a culture shock, especially if their new homes are subjected to armed raids or they are held up in the street.

Jamaica is no longer the sleepy rural island they left, and some complain that they are made to feel unwelcome by the "real" Jamaicans they have returned to live among. Poor health care and social services also become a key factor when older returnees find their health and mobility deteriorating. Although many stay and make a success of the move, some re-emigrate within a year or so of coming back.

Crime

Crime, and fear of crime, is a major preoccupation in Jamaica; its ramifications are inescapable and, despite the efforts of some politicians, are difficult to play down. Tourism and investment suffer in equal measures from the negative image and instability that high crime rates engender.

Reported crime levels actually began to fall in the late 1990s, partly because more resources were pumped into policing. But murder rates show no signs of falling, and in fact steadily increased by about ten percent a year from 1990 to 1997. On average, there are more than 1,000 murders each year, twice the number in the UK, which has a population 20 times as big. Most are the result of gunplay, and more than two-thirds are committed in the Kingston area.

There are many theories as to why Jamaica should be plagued by violence when other democratic Caribbean countries are far more peaceful, but one of the key factors is the lethal combination of a large gap between rich and poor and the easy availability of guns. Since the 1970s, when the current wave of violent crime began, guns have been easy to acquire either legally through permits from the police or illegally on the streets. Their presence in the volatile atmosphere of the Kingston ghettos, where the only option for many young men is to turn to crime, guarantees serious trouble on a depressingly regular basis.

Hardly a day goes by without newspaper reports of two or three shot dead in gunfights, and the recent arrival of the South American cocaine trade, which uses Jamaica as a shipment point for the US, has increased the turmoil. Gangs that once fought to control the indigenous marijuana business now battle for their share of the pass-through trade in cocaine and crack, which find their way on to the domestic market and – through internal trading and addiction – create more violent crime.

The National Council on Drug Abuse runs drug abuse prevention programs in schools and is trying to work on ways of providing economic stability for recovering addicts and marginalized youths, but it is fighting an uphill battle. In 1997 the narcotics division of the Ministry of National Security arrested 7,352 people for trafficking and possession of illicit drugs.

Reputations count for everything on the streets of Kingston as "dons" or "generals" in various territories try to out-vie each other in reprisal killings or audacious raids designed to undermine their rivals. Few big players last long in such a precarious world, but the frequent deaths of young men in their prime lend a semi-mythical status to the victims that encourages other ghetto youths to follow in their footsteps. To make things worse, gangster culture is often exacerbated by hardened emigrants who feed back into the ghetto after being deported for misdemeanors in the US. About 5,500 were sent back to Jamaica between 1996 and 1998 alone.

The response of the hard-pressed and well-armed Jamaica Constabulary Force is usually to meet fire with fire. The police have a fearful reputation for shooting first and asking questions later, and there are widespread allegations that officers prefer to take out troublemakers than to rely on a rickety legal system to imprison them. More than 100 people were shot and killed by police every year in the late 1990s, with a total of 145 in 1998, the second highest figure in Latin America and the Caribbean.

Internal investigations of police shootings are often cursory and usually accept the official version that officers have returned fire after being ambushed. The cry of "police murder" is so commonplace in the ghettos that it is difficult to separate genuine grievances from those that are not, but deaths involving police action are way above those to be found in any other democratic society in the Western Hemisphere.

The Jamaica Defence Force, which was founded in 1962 as an all-in-one armed force covering land air and sea, is also called upon to deal with serious breakdowns in law and order or to help with special operations in ghetto areas. Although it has no powers of arrest, it too has become embroiled in controversy – notably in 1997, when four women and a six-year-old boy were shot dead during a JDF helicopter raid on the Jamaica Labour Party "garrison" of Tivoli Gardens in Kingston.

Police pre-occupations with high-profile shootings and ghetto warfare mean that the time for addressing other crimes is reduced – and ensures that the dishing out of punishment by vigilante mobs is a continuing problem. Street robbers and other offenders are hacked or beaten to death at the rate of about 20 a year, yet perpetrators are rarely brought to justice, as local communities close ranks.

Many households in Kingston have decided to take crime prevention into their own hands by having at least one revolver or shotgun in their home for "self-defense," along with a couple of fierce dogs, walls studded with broken glass, and bars on the windows. Until guns are taken out of the system and social problems caused by poverty are ameliorated, there is little prospect of this siege mentality lifting, at least in the capital.

Human Rights

The Jamaican response to violent crime has created a negative image of the island abroad. Amnesty International has complained of "continuing evidence that human rights are violated in Jamaica with alarming frequency," and human rights observers have had cause for concern about a number of issues on the island over recent years, most notably the use of the death penalty and the activities of the police.

Dozens of death sentences are handed out each year by courts that are increasingly desperate to exert some control over the spiraling murder rate. At any one time there are about 45 people on death row, although internal and external pressure has led many sentences to be commuted to life imprisonment, and the last execution took place in 1988. Nevertheless, Amnesty International says that there are grave concerns about the safety of trials that lead to death sentences, as well as the lack of time for appeals to be heard.

Successive governments have shown growing determination over recent years to ignore international condemnation and go ahead with hangings. In 1998 Jamaica became the first country ever to withdraw from the optional protocol to the International Covenant on Civil and Political Rights, which acts as an avenue of appeal for those trying to avoid the death penalty. The move caused outrage abroad and theoretically left Jamaican citizens with no way of seeking redress for alleged violations of their rights. Yet public support for the death penalty is strong, and the government's increasingly hard-line approach has received widespread backing. Executions continue to be postponed at the last minute, but it may only be a matter of time before hangings become a reality again.

Other aspects of the Jamaican legal system are also condemned abroad. Flogging by tamarind switch can still be ordered, although this punishment has not been seen for many years, and sex in private between consenting male adults is illegal, with the crime of sodomy punishable by up to ten years imprisonment with hard labor. Prejudice against homosexuals in Jamaica is aggressively rife, as reggae singer Buju Nanton reflected in his hit song *Boom Bye Bye*, which suggested that gays should be shot whenever possible. Liberalization of the law is not even on the agenda.

Ill-treatment by prison and police officers, deaths in police and prison custody, and the use of firearms by police have all been raised as unacceptable aspects of Jamaica's human rights situation – especially as few alleged incidents are satisfactorily investigated by the authorities. Poor ghetto dwellers are often detained in police custody beyond the statutory two days, denied access to lawyers, and subjected to beatings.

Prison conditions have been described by the Human Rights Committee as "appalling," with frequent serious mistreatment of prisoners, many prisoner-on-prisoner killings inside jails, overcrowding, poor diet, unsatisfactory sanitary conditions, and insufficient medical care. The General Penitentiary near Kingston's harbor is notorious, with periodic disturbances and prisoner-on-prisoner killings.

On the judicial front, the international community is also critical of a legal system – based on the British one, wigs and all – that is inefficient and clogged with cases. Trials are often delayed for up to two years, many are abandoned because files are lost, and the courts are generally overburdened. On the other hand, there are also worries about rushed cases carried through without legal aid – especially those leading to the death penalty.

Election time abuses of human rights have, however, reduced considerably since the 1970s, and Jamaica has a generally good record on academic and press freedom as well as religious tolerance.

TV, Newspapers and Radio

The media is now multifaceted, although dominated by the US. There are three morning newspapers, all sold on the street by vendors and all prepared to criticize the government: the *Jamaica Herald*, the conservative leaning *Daily Gleaner* (founded 1834), and the *Jamaica Observer*. The owners of the *Daily Gleaner* also publish an afternoon tabloid called *The Star.*

The healthy radio scene offers eight stations, including the popular reggae-based Irie FM and a religious station called Love FM. Much of the radio fare is made up of talk shows, celebrity gossip, or advice lines, and is hugely popular for it. The Jamaica Broadcasting Company (JBC) has run a television station since 1963 and since March 1993 has had a rival in CVM TV, which takes advertisements and relies heavily on US imports. Rather stilted public information slots appear regularly on TV and radio, courtesy of the government's Jamaica Information Service.

Zion healing mission   *Marc French/Panos Pictures*

Low-cost TV feeds and agency news copy from the US make it cheaper for Jamaican news gatherers to re-hash US news than to dig out original stories on their own doorstep – as the dominance of the O.J. Simpson murder case revealed in the mid-1990s. Trashy one-episode-a-day soap operas such as *The Young and the Restless* rule the roost, and there is even a local potboiler called *Royal Palm Estates*. Jamaican TV and radio presenters use American program styling and pronunciations, R&B and hip hop dominate the radio waves, and although the print media retains slightly more of a Caribbean feel, newspapers give a lot of space to American basketball and football reports.

Satellite TV is now theoretically accessible to even the most remote rural shack and even those who only have the core of terrestrial TV channels will spend most of the time watching American programming. Radio remains the best feasible option for most poor people, however.

Religion

Religion is one of the strongest social forces in Jamaican life. Every Sunday morning villages and small towns on the island come to a standstill as men and boys in suits and women and girls in broad-brimmed hats, lace dresses, and white stockings make their way to worship. Jamaica has the highest number of churches per person in the world, with more than 100 Christian denominations and a correspondingly high rate of churchgoing.

About seven percent of the population is officially Catholic (a hangover from Spanish rule) and there are tiny Jewish, Hindu, and Muslim communities, but the vast majority, about 80 percent, subscribe to various Protestant faiths that have synthesized white European Christianity with the remnants of black West African faiths. The Anglican church, in the shape of the Church of Jamaica, remains fairly strong from the days of British influence, but the Baptists and Methodists have hundreds of thousands of adherents. The Church of God is now hugely influential and there are thousands more Moravians, Pentecostalists, Presbyterians, Seventh Day Adventists, and Jehovah's Witnesses. Even in urban areas and among elite circles, it is rare to find many people who do not have a strong Christian faith, even if they do not go to church. Most Jamaicans, young or small, can quote large passages of the bible by heart.

The island has long been fertile ground for fiery preachers, and for many Jamaicans a strong church represents one of the few moral buffers against the crime and corruption they perceive all around them. In recent years, under the influence of TV stations beamed from the US and relatives returning from North America, fundamentalist and evangelical Christianity has boomed. This spiritual import has fueled the propensity of some Jamaicans to favor a peculiarly apocalyptic strain of Protestantism that often shows itself in the popularity of proverbs, visions, strict interpretation of the biblical prophesies, and predictions of Armageddon. Churches such as the Salvation Army and the Christian Scientists have won many converts with moral stances that tie in closely with traditional Jamaican feelings on issues such as homosexuality and the importance of family life.

In the rural areas that are generally the strongholds of churchgoing, the power of religion can be seen most strikingly as absurdly over-amplified preachers conduct two or three hour services in front of sweating congregations who sing, sway, dance, clap their hands, and, depending on their proclivities, faint from spirit possession. Jamaicans take their religion seriously, but they have fun with it too. Jamaican women in particular derive special comfort and spiritual sustenance from the church. They are the backbone of church organization, making up the majority in most congregations and in some, such as the Pentecostalists, perhaps up to three-quarters of the attendance.

Jamaica was not always so: with its worldly white colonists and a slave population deemed to be unworthy of conversion, the island was fallow ground for Christianity until the end of the eighteenth century, when the first missionaries began to instruct slaves on sugar estates owned by Moravian families in St. Elizabeth. A period of religious revivalism in the late 1800s led to a rapid growth in churches as the black population, with its enthusiasm for singing, shouting, and dancing, quickly diverged from the staid norms expected by the white Anglicans.

Baptism became particularly strong among the ex-slaves after emancipation, for it encouraged the development of black preachers. Baptist churches encouraged a self-help ethic and were generally a social force for good. These days they boast collective membership of around 300,000 people, with Methodism claiming another 250,000.

Echoes of Africa

African religions were eroded from an early stage by planter hostility, by syncretism with Christianity, and by the fact that there was no commonly held dogma among a slave population that hailed from many different cultural regions of West Africa.

Although most churchgoing is suffused to some extent with the remnants of African religion, its impact has been nowhere near as great as in, say, Haiti, where *vodoun* (voodoo) is so strong. On the other hand, some Jamaican sects have managed to preserve relatively strong links with African ancestral worship. Kumina, in particular, has survived in its heartland of St. Thomas, where small numbers of people continue to worship ancestral spirits who take possession of the living. Adherents worship through an inspirational mix of dancing and drumming that has partly been kept alive by the National Dance Theatre Company.

The related Pocomania is a similar, although slightly more urban and Christianized sect that involves the singing of hymns and the use of drums to induce spirit possession (popularly known as "jumping"). More generally, some Jamaicans also still practice Obeah, a catch-all term for relics of West African beliefs that can vary from herbalism and "bush medicine" to the casting of spells that affect the behavior of others. In a firmly Christian society, Obeah has the same negative connotations as witchcraft in Europe, but it is also treated with a healthy amount of respect, especially in rural areas. Many ordinary churchgoers are not above turning to an Obeah man or women if they believe bad spells have been cast against them or if they want to improve their luck, especially when it comes to encouraging interest from the opposite sex.

West African beliefs also remain on a folkloric level in the popular oral tales of Anancy, the trickster spider, and in the widespread belief in ghosts or "duppies," shapeshifters, and bloodsuckers.

Rastafarianism

For many across the world, however, Jamaica is most associated with Rastafarianism, a contrary faith that originated just before the Second World War and is now thought to be followed by at least 100,000 people world-wide.

Known principally for the dreadlocks of its followers and their attachment to ganja – as well as its links with the reggae musician Bob Marley and its belief in the divinity of the Ethiopian emperor Haile Selassie,

Rastafari emerged during the 1930s from Jamaica's strong Ethiopianist movement, which had been drawing a biblical link between black people and Ethiopians as the descendants of the Israelites since the early half of the 1800s.

Although it made use of the secular ideas of black intellectuals such as the pan-Africanist Dr. Robert Love, the anti-colonialist Dr. Theophilus Scholes, and Marcus Garvey, it was the more down-to-earth preacher Leonard Howell – often dubbed "the first Rastafari" – who talked specifically of the biblical significance of Haile Selassie. When Selassie, as Ras Makonnen, was crowned Emperor of Ethiopia in 1930, Howell pointed out that his title, King of Kings, Lord of Lords, appeared in the Book of Revelations and that the new emperor's lineage could be traced back to King Solomon and the Queen of Sheba, effectively making him the son of God. Here was a new messiah, a Ras Tafari ("black king") ready to deliver black people from their suffering.

Howell's ideas coincided with a period of renewed religious fervor in Jamaica, and his Rasta message found ready converts in the poorest areas of Kingston and nearby St. Thomas. Playing the role of prophet among the squatter communities of the capital, he tapped into the deep disillusionment of a people long accustomed to searching the bible for explanations of their plight and hints of their salvation. At the very least, many poor Jamaicans felt proud to follow the fortunes of a black emperor who commanded respect on the world stage – and when the Italians invaded Ethiopia in 1935, interest in Selassie increased still further.

In 1940 Howell set up a Rasta commune at Pinnacle, near Sligoville, which survived more than a decade of police harassment, until he was arrested and packed off to a mental institution in 1955. The surviving members drifted into the poorest parts of Kingston to form new Rasta enclaves in slums such as Back 'o' Wall, spreading the message and gathering new recruits.

Despite their generally peaceful nature, Rastas were viewed by most Jamaicans during this early period as a sinister threat to public decency, a ganja-crazed danger to children and the moral fabric of society. The police, with government sanction, treated them as public enemy number one, incarcerating them and shaving their hair, bulldozing their communities and even, on occasions, challenging them in spectacular gunfights.

By the middle of the 1960s, however, the tide was beginning to turn as the youth of Jamaica, urged on by emerging musicians such as Bob Marley, started to see the sense in a Rasta perspective that neatly analyzed their plight, spoke directly to them, and was undeniably attractive, not least in its use of ganja.

Bob Marley statue near the national stadium   *Ian Cumming*

When the diminutive Selassie visited Jamaica as part of a Caribbean tour in 1966, the response was overwhelming. Kingston airport was besieged by huge crowds curious to see whether Selassie really was the incarnation of God or "Jah." The excitement that accompanied his visit added many more followers to what was already a fast growing movement. Selassie himself was mystified and slightly concerned at the elevated status he had been given, but the Rasta train had long since pulled out of the station.

Even the politicians, most notably Michael Manley, started to weave Rasta expressions and concepts into their rhetoric, and as Bob Marley's increasingly international fame spread the doctrine throughout the world, Jamaica was forced to reassess Rastafari's legitimacy. Almost overnight – and despite the death of Selassie in 1975, Rastafarianism gained a credibility that the likes of Howell could never have expected. Dreadlocks and the Rasta lifestyle became fashionable, and pseudo-Rastas (disparagingly known by the real thing as "wolves") dressed up to impress tourists on the north coast. Rasta also became a religious export as thousands in the Jamaican diaspora (and elsewhere in the Caribbean) identified with the fight against a materialistic white "Babylon" committed to oppressing black people.

Since the heyday of the 1970s and early 1980s, Rastafari has commanded rather less attention in Jamaica, and although still strong, it has struggled to find a unifying philosophy or leading figure. There are now a number of different factions within Rastafarianism, including the relatively liberal Twelve Tribes of Israel and the more hard-line, reclusive Bobo Shanti. Some Rastas have moved toward the Ethiopian Orthodox Church while others have even jumped ship to embrace mainstream Christianity, much to the annoyance of a younger generation of hard-core Rastas who like to predict "fire burn" for those who turn the wrong way.

Due partly to the fact that Rastafari was undermined by part-timers who adopted a selective approach to its various tenets, the definition of the faith and its facets has become more fluid. At its strictest, Rasta prohibits the use of alcohol, tobacco, or hard drugs, and prescribes an "ital" diet that is salt-free, vegan, and organic. Yet it is by no means uncommon to see a "locksman" sipping on a bottle of Red Stripe beer while tucking into a hamburger. As in any faith, there are those who prefer to make their own interpretations of how they should be running their lives.

Likewise, few Rastas have ever opted to move to Africa, preferring instead to see Ethiopia as a spiritual homeland or fabled "Zion" that provides a comforting anchor, even if they never intend to go there. While ganja smoking, either socially or at prayerful *nyabinghi* gatherings, remains perhaps the most sturdy of the faith's foundations, not even dreadlocks are regarded as a prerequisite these days, and there are some Rastas who are even willing to question the divinity of Haile Selassie. Whether Rastafarianism is actually a religion rather than a set of beliefs is up for debate – even within the Rasta community.

What has survived is a complicated mix of back-to-Africanism, black consciousness, moral teachings drawn from the bible, anti-establishment rhetoric, and belief in the insightful power of ganja. Many Rastas have been highly political (with a small "p"), but most have rejected the idea of spreading their message through Jamaican mainstream "politricks" or the workings of Babylon. Instead, they have concentrated on the fields of music, arts, and community organization, to which they have made a healthy contribution and through which they have garnered much support in Jamaica and the wider world.

5   ECONOMY: ELUSIVE RICHES

Compared with many smaller Caribbean islands that have done well for themselves with tourism and little else, Jamaica – with its sugar, bananas, bauxite, tourism, and modest manufacturing sector – has a relatively diversified economy that should, in theory, provide a basis for prosperity. In practice, however, Jamaica has known nothing but economic heartache and under-performance for years, and shows few signs of being able to put an end to the distress in the near future, despite being well endowed with natural resources.

For a short spell after independence, as the economic policies of Norman Manley and Bustamante exploited bauxite on a large scale for the first time, things appeared to be going fairly well. Gross Domestic Product (GDP) grew at about five percent per year from 1962 to 1973 and there was optimism in many quarters. But this newly created wealth was spread unevenly across the economy or was leaching out of the country to foreign investors. While some Jamaicans were making a fortune, the majority continued in desperate circumstances, subject to the huge income disparities that have remained one of Jamaica's biggest social and economic problems to this day.

When the oil crisis and international recession of the 1970s hit Jamaica, any progress that had been made in the immediate post-independence period quickly disappeared under Michael Manley and Edward Seaga. External debt mushroomed, foreign investors fled, trade deficits grew, currency crises abounded, inflation ran at about 30 percent and unemployment reached new highs. The economy quite simply fell apart.

The road back to some semblance of economic stability has been a long and painful one since then, played out against a backdrop of retrenchment, privatization, and free-market trickle-down economics. Matters were made immeasurably worse by the devastation of Hurricane Gilbert in 1988, whose 125 mph winds set the economy back years with a death toll of 45, half a million made homeless, and a repair bill of $50 million. In some parts of the island, electricity did not return for more than a year.

Although by 1999 inflation had dropped to the relatively low level of 8 percent after averaging 36 percent between 1990 and 1996, the economy is still inherently shaky. This is especially true in the financial sector, where the government has stepped in with billions of Jamaican dollars to bail out collapsed local banks and insurance companies. While money is diverted from social programs to prop up financial institutions, there is

Coronation market,
Kingston

Marc French/Panos Pictures

still little cash filtering down to the poor, who are virtually powerless to keep up with the ever-rising cost of living. Roadblocks and violent demonstrations almost always accompany painful new economic measures, as they did in the 1999 protests against a proposed rise in gasoline tax, when three days of rioting left nine dead and virtually shut down the country.

Annual average incomes on the island are hardly impressive at $2,170, yet even that mean is distorted by the vast gap in incomes. Most people earn far less. The official unemployment rate has been running at about 17 percent for years, with even higher rates among women and young people. The majority of jobless people, unskilled in an economy that suffers from a skills shortage, have to rely on work in the informal sector for whatever income they can find.

Higglers

Higglers are a key feature of Jamaica's informal economy. Often middle-aged women who occupy regular spots in and around urban markets, they usually work on their own, or perhaps with children, selling agricultural produce such as fruits and vegetables or sweets and snacks.

Traditionally, higglers have hailed from the villages outside Kingston and the other urban centers, but increasingly poor town dwellers have also turned their hand to pavement selling. Now every town boasts an ever-growing number of sidewalk vendors offering not just food, but cigarettes, trinkets, and cheap imported clothing. They often set up outside shops as well as in the markets of Kingston.

Some estimates have suggested there are at least 15,000 higglers working in Kingston alone, supporting about 68,000 people with their incomes. For many women, higglering is one of the few ways of providing income to bring up their children in the absence of a supportive male. Some hope that it will be an entrepreneurial way out of poverty, but for many others it is merely a temporary way of staving off destitution, an alternative to unemployment, or a way of avoiding back-breaking domestic work.

Very few earn much money, especially as earnings habitually have to be invested in buying new stock. Yet higglers are frequently targeted by politicians, who blame them for undercutting commercial businesses or creating a nuisance – and make heavy capital out of those few entrepreneurs who have taken higglering to a higher plane by traveling abroad to Panama or Haiti to stock up on cheap consumer goods. There are periodic sweeps of the streets to disperse pavement sellers, which polls show have general support from the public, even though many consumers use higglers on a regular basis.

Bauxite

If there is one unquestionably ugly thing in the beautiful countryside of Jamaica, it is the unsightly red gashes of the bauxite mines that tear open the landscape around the central towns of Mandeville, Christiana, and Ewarton. For most Jamaicans, though, the mines are a sight for sore eyes. Bauxite, the raw material for aluminum, has been a godsend to Jamaica, even if it has not quite been its savior.

Raw bauxite and its more refined cousin, alumina, are the country's biggest money makers, earning about half of its export income each year ($755 million in 1997 out of total exports of $1.4 billion) and, through the bauxite levy, acting as a handy source of tax revenue for the government. With estimated reserves of up to three billion tons, the central economic role of Jamaica's "red gold" is likely to continue for many years to come.

Yet despite record production levels of bauxite in recent years, Jamaica has found it difficult to cope with cheap competition from South America and Australia. The industry held its own in the 1990s, but in the 1980s, when prices fell world-wide, it contracted sharply and the economy was severely undermined as a result. More frustratingly, none of the alumina or bauxite is actually turned into aluminum on the island, which means that Jamaica misses out on the most lucrative part of the aluminum industry. Manufacturing aluminum requires large amounts of cheap fuel, which Jamaica does not have; in the absence of its own oil resources, it has to watch helplessly while other countries add significant value to its raw material.

Because bauxite extraction relies heavily on machinery, it also supports only about 6,000 jobs, or just one percent of the employed labor force – with the result that its immediate benefits to the wider population are limited. Foreign firms, such as Alcoa (US) and Alcan (Canada) also continue to dominate many of the operations.

Decent reserves of gypsum, marble, high-grade calcium carbonate, clay, and silica are offering other increasingly lucrative opportunities for mineral

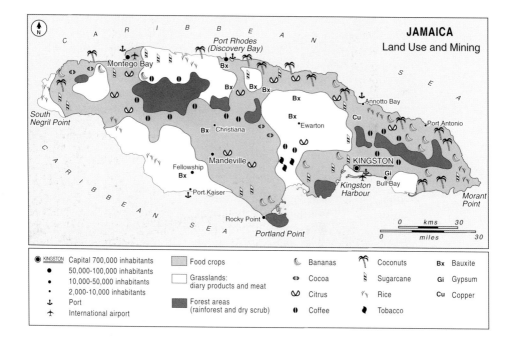

extraction by local firms, and there are vast amounts of limestone yet to be tapped.

Manufacturing

Since the 1950s Jamaica has made a big effort to foster a viable manufacturing industry, and as a relatively large island with a reasonably sized domestic market it has made some headway. Its manufacturing sector accounts for between 10 and 15 percent of employment and about a fifth of GDP.

Factories in the industrial areas of Kingston and Montego Bay produce a wide variety of consumer goods, especially clothes and textiles, and can attract foreign investment with some of the cheapest labor in the Caribbean. A low-tech, but well-respected, reggae recording industry churns out exports of vinyl from small units and recording studios. Tens of thousands of workers also find employment in three "free zones" – one of them near Kingston's harbor – where there are tax concessions, no unions, and few red tape inconveniences such as factory inspections. Companies from the US, Taiwan, and Hong Kong set up in the zones with regularity.

Women workers leaving the
Free Trade Zone, Kingston

Marc French/Panos Pictures

Things have rarely been easy, however, and despite the benefits of Caricom membership, which has opened up a useful export market, the manufacturing sector has been in a lull for some years – hit by cheaper imports, high interest rates, inflation, and the rising cost of imported raw materials. Given that the unions have just fifteen percent membership across the national workforce, and that management styles are often provocative, lay-offs common, and salaries poor (the minimum wage is $22.50 per week), expensive and disruptive industrial disputes are also commonplace.

Agriculture

During the cane-cutting season, the clear air of rural parishes such as St. Catherine and Clarendon is regularly filled with flecks of ash from canefields that have been set alight to clear scrub, while the roads are littered with charred cane that has fallen from trucks rushing to deliver their loads for processing. Sugar may no longer be king in Jamaica, but it is still the most important agricultural product in the country, and is second only to bauxite as a foreign currency earner.

Many of the old plantations still exist, including the oldest and most famous of them all, the Appleton estate near Maggotty in St. Elizabeth. Dating back to 1655, when the British arrived, it has a factory unit that can produce up to 160 tons of sugar a day and a rum distillery that uses

Cane cutters, late 19th century

Courtesy of John Gilmore

molasses to produce ten million liters of rum a year under the Appleton and Wray & Nephew brands.

About half of all Jamaica's sugar is still grown on large estates, but most are nowhere near as high-tech as Appleton, and the rest are cultivated by small landowners who generally sell to factories through cooperatives. Most government-owned sugar mills were privatized in 1993, but the government was forced to repurchase some of its holdings in 1998 after disastrous losses, due largely to drought, threatened to close the mills. Most of Jamaica's sugar is exported to the European Union or the US under preferential trading agreements, which earned the island $73 million in 1997.

Jamaica's other main crop is bananas, which were introduced in the sixteenth century but never wholly established themselves until the 1950s, when the British government decided that a substantial banana crop could help produce much needed diversification. Many small farmers in Jamaica cultivate bananas, but the most important growers are the larger estates in the high rainfall areas of St. Mary and Portland.

Banana growing is vulnerable to periodic setbacks due to outbreaks of disease and hurricane damage (Hurricane Gilbert wiped out the entire export crop in 1988). But the greatest threat in recent times has come from a successful campaign by US banana multinationals (such as Chiquita) to end the EU quotas that guaranteed a market for Jamaican and other Caribbean suppliers.

Coffee is also under pressure, even though Jamaica's superb Blue Mountain variety is among the smoothest and most expensive in the world. Poor organization, corruption, and the proliferation of small-time coffee growers on the slopes of the mountains have led to overall inefficiency and confusion. Many growers sell their coffee to the government-run Coffee Industry Board, which has been in financial crisis for a number of years and has sometimes had difficulty paying for crops. Some farmers have been calling for a government bail-out.

Cocoa, oranges, tobacco, and spices such as ginger and pimento also earn modest export income, while "provisions" such as yams, sweet potatoes, pumpkins, and plantain are mainly grown on small plots for home use or the domestic market.

Marijuana is also a significant source of illegal income for many farmers, who hide lucrative crops of especially strong and prized "sensimilla" deep in the bush or on remote hillsides. The authorities, under continual pressure from the US government, hunt out and ritually burn hundreds of acres of ganja each year, intercept consignments at makeshift airfields or, more problematically, try to cut off high-speed motorboats used to run the crop into Florida.

In general, the contribution of agriculture to the economy has risen slightly in recent years – in contrast to the 1970s and 1980s, when the political initiative was toward industry and manufacturing. Agriculture earns about $200 million in foreign exchange each year and as the country's second largest employer by sector (after tourism) it provides jobs, one way or the other, for more than 200,000 people.

Tourism

Of the many gifts Jamaica has brought the world, one of the most unlikely – and controversial – has been the concept of the all-inclusive resort. With their one-fee-for-everything approach and their guarded compounds where sun-seekers chill out in blissful ignorance of the harsh reality outside, all-inclusives are perhaps an inevitable result of the Jamaican juxtaposition of beautiful beaches and social instability.

The white Jamaican entrepreneur Gordon "Butch" Stewart is generally credited with kicking off the concept when he started his all-inclusive Sandals resort in Montego Bay in 1981, shortly to be followed by fellow businessman John Issa, who set up Super Clubs. At a time when tourists were being deterred from visiting Jamaica because of its fierce reputation for political violence and gang warfare, all-inclusives revitalized the tourist industry with their idea that visitors could be flown straight in to Montego Bay, bussed into a plush compound and have all their needs attended to without having to venture into the potentially hostile atmosphere beyond.

Since those early beginnings, all-inclusives have spread like wildfire across the north coast and have proved to be a raging success all over the

58

Doctor's cave bathing beach, Montego Bay, c1940s   *Courtesy of John Gilmore*

Caribbean, even in countries with no need to shelter tourists from potential trouble. Chiefly patronized by tourists from the US and Europe, they are a relatively cheap, convenient, and enjoyable way of spending two weeks in the sun with access to free food and drink, private beaches, and unlimited sporting activities such as water sports, golf and tennis.

All-inclusives are, in fact, one of the few Jamaican success stories of recent years, and have made rich and influential people out of the likes of Butch Stewart, who now also owns the privatized national airline, Air Jamaica (2,000 employees) and the local *Observer* newspaper. But they are not without their critics, especially among those Jamaicans inclined to perceive them as a kind of apartheid structure that keeps the locals separate from the "rich" outsiders.

Although many wrist-tagged all-inclusive customers do venture out from their resorts to visit the sights, there is little incentive to go far or to spend money elsewhere when they can get everything free back in the compound. Craft sellers and vendors who try to make an independent living from tourism often complain that the immediate local economy is left high and dry while the likes of Sandals, Couples, and Jamaica Grande corner the market. There is also inevitable resentment at the them-and-us feeling that the all-inclusives tend to create, as bikini-clad whites stroll around inside the perimeter fences in seeming indifference to the poverty outside.

The stark reality, however, is that without all-inclusives and the sense of safety they generate, Jamaican tourism would probably be far less successful. More than one million tourists visit the island each year, making

Marriage on the beach, Negril   *Ian Cumming*

it the second biggest destination in the Caribbean after the Bahamas. Tourism pumped more than $1 billion into the economy in 1998, and the all-inclusives account for a large proportion of the 45 percent of the country's foreign exchange earned by tourism.

What is more, they have kept the tourist industry largely in local hands, with 90 percent of hotels Jamaican-owned. Tourism employs about 84,000 people directly, with perhaps a further 170,000 indirectly making a living from it, and it keeps many local farmers in business supplying food to hotels and resort complexes.

Despite some seasonal fluctuations and occasional setbacks when outbreaks of violence hit bookings, tourism has held up reasonably well since the boom of the late 1980s and has been important in sheltering Jamaica from over-reliance on sugar and bauxite. There have been big improvements in infrastructure on the north coast and some successful moves to counteract localized crime and harassment, as well as a significant expansion in the number of hotels. Good marketing has kept the island competitive on the world market (Sandals has an annual advertising budget ten times that of the Jamaica Tourist Board), and while the number of up-market cruise ship visits has more than doubled since the beginning of the 1990s, Jamaica has simultaneously presented itself as a favored cheap holiday venue for American college students on their spring break and as an increasingly popular setting for combined weddings and honeymoons (Sandals organizes 2,000 a year alone). Three-quarters of visitors come from the US or Canada, with most of the rest from Europe and increasing numbers from Japan, as well as 100,000 Jamaicans each year from the diaspora.

Some Jamaicans still nurse resentment against tourism, seeing it as an extension of black servitude to the rich white world. But attitudes have changed dramatically over the past 20 years, partly aided by government education initiatives. Recent surveys have shown higher job satisfaction among Jamaicans in the hotel industry than anywhere else.

Besides, there has been some internal recognition of the drawbacks of all-inclusive resorts and the quick stopover cruise ships. In 1999 the Jamaica Tourist Board launched an "Insider's Jamaica" program designed to provide an alternative to the all-inclusives by featuring small local hotels and car rental deals that offer tourists the chance of visiting the island more independently. There are also moves to open up the south coast and an ambitious scheme to market Jamaica's heritage by raising the old Port Royal from the sea, though the project has already had several false dawns.

Debt

Recent PNP governments have set themselves firmly against a return to the days when Jamaica borrowed so much that it was virtually beholden to the International Monetary Fund and the World Bank. Local politicians finally got the IMF off their backs in September 1995 after eighteen years of repayments and austerity programs, but the debt problem has by no means gone away, and is still an enormous burden. External debt stood at $3.9 billion in 1998 – or about $1,500 per person in Jamaica – and domestic borrowing has also mushroomed. Debt servicing took up a crippling two-thirds of the government's 1999 budget, leaving little room for spending on education, health, and social services.

Under the circumstances – and with overseas aid falling – it is by no means certain that any Jamaican government will be able to resist going back to the IMF, however much it might like to stay away. Matters have not been helped by a crisis in the financial sector which began in 1996. When the government created the Financial Sector Adjustment Company (FINSAC) in 1997 to engineer bailouts of failing banks and insurance companies, it committed itself overnight to massively increased state indebtedness. Many of the half dozen or so banks it has taken over have struggled to produce any improvement in their fortunes, which were destroyed by bad management, risky lending, corruption, and poorly secured loans. Large numbers of Jamaicans lost their life savings in bank collapses,

Extracting river sand from the Rio Grande   *John Gilmore*

regardless of FINSAC's intervention. Many now prefer to put their money into foreign-owned banks for safety.

Infrastructure

The lack of state funds for public spending has severely hampered development of the country's infrastructure outside of the north coast. Travel by car or lorry is arduous, for there are few well-kept roads or two-lane highways anywhere, and most business people fly the short distance from Montego to Kingston to save time. The roads have struggled to cope with a big increase in car-use since the government relaxed rules on the import of environmentally outmoded Japanese vehicles, known colloquially as "deportees." Kingston, in particular, suffers from big traffic jams at rush hour times, as well as increasing pollution. Driving is dangerous, too: accident rates and deaths on the road are disturbingly high.

For the poor, the buses are woefully inadequate and, given the limited earning capacity of those who travel on them, overpriced. Services are generally acknowledged to have deteriorated since recent privatization, with badly maintained ex-US school buses full to bursting point at most times of the day (especially in Kingston), and time tables virtually non-existent.

The British built 229 miles of railway during their stay, including a picturesque line from Kingston to Montego Bay, but after years of neglect most of the track has disappeared, with only a few short stretches maintained by the aluminum companies to service the bauxite mines. Although there are long-standing plans to reinstate the railway as a quick and efficient link across country, the cost of doing so is now so prohibitive that there is little likelihood of it happening. Apart perhaps from the dubiously beneficial growth of privately financed shopping malls with Dunkin' Donuts and McDonalds outlets, the only other bright spot on the infrastructure front is the recently modernized and privatized telephone system, which now runs more efficiently in the hands of Cable & Wireless.

The Environment

The state of Jamaica's struggling economy has reduced environmental issues to a low priority as the country strives for prosperity rather than a reputation for ecological consciousness.

Most of the island's previously extensive coral reefs have all but gone, due to fishing, careless tourist development, and sea pollution. Deforestation has been especially prevalent in the Blue Mountains, with ramifications for many of the low-lying parts of the southeast, such as Yallahs, where there have been long-standing problems with soil erosion. Bauxite mining disfigures and pollutes large tracts of land, although some exhausted acres are now being reinstated as cattle grazing lands. Poor infrastructure means that waste disposal is also a major irritant, with dumping commonplace even in some of the most beautiful spots.

The rather toothless National Resource Conservation Authority was created in 1991 to try to improve the environment, and in 1996 an environmental policy was announced as one of four main planks of a long-term national industrial policy for economic growth. A subsequent national environmental action plan has focused on land use and watershed management, including hillside erosion, and pollution of water from sewage and the bauxite industry. Despite the difficulties, however, Jamaica's relative under-development has spared the countryside from the worst excesses that quick economic growth often brings.

6 CULTURE: ON THE WORLD STAGE

In spite of – or more likely because of – the well-chronicled difficulties attached to everyday living in Jamaica, its people revel in a rich and inventive cultural life that helps to compensate for at least some of the hardships. Jamaica's travails have helped to fuel tremendous creativity and achievement in music, sport and the arts, where success offers one of the few ways out of ghetto life. They have also been the source of inspiration for generations of musicians, writers and artists eager either to kick back against the system or just to escape for a time into a world where things seem less troubled. In a society where the poor have few formal means of expression or advancement, reggae and cricket in particular have given millions of Jamaicans the freedom to shape something in their own image – and to wield an astonishing amount of influence on the cultural life of the rest of the world.

Reggae

Reggae is without doubt Jamaica's most recognizable and significant cultural asset. Its rhythm has spread worldwide over the past four decades in a way that few other musical forms have ever been able to achieve. Although it has been a commercial success, it has been a spiritual one too, adopted as the music of the dispossessed in many corners of the third world, from Latin America to Africa.

Jamaicans are fond of claiming they produce a greater output of recorded music per head than any other nation in the world, and it is easy to believe. Although much of the music business on the island is run on an *ad hoc*, exploitative, shoestring basis – and is still focused mainly around records rather than CDs – prodigious amounts of musical product are pushed out from small studios and record pressers every week, catering to the almost insatiable demands of the Jamaican public. In a musical scene based around the huge sound systems that blast out the latest music in the most basic of dancehalls or empty lots, reggae is driven by an overwhelming desire to find the next rhythm, the next dance style, or the next DJ superstar.

All sorts of internal musical influences have contributed to reggae, but its origins lie principally in black American R&B, which began to reach the island after the Second World War via radio or records from the US. Jamaican musicians who were more used to playing the folk-based, calypso-like *mento* began to copy, then adapt, the R&B style for local audiences who gathered in the open air "lawns" and dancehalls of Kingston to hear the latest sounds from America. Traveling sound systems run by the legendary Duke Reid and his rival Clement "Coxsone" Dodd vied to find and play the latest imports from the US until, in the late 1950s, local entrepreneurs (including Edward Seaga) financed the birth of a Jamaican recording industry that began to produce material by home-grown talent.

By 1958 local singer Laurel Aitken had managed to produce a number one Jamaican hit as others, led by Prince Buster, almost imperceptibly changed the R&B beat into a faster, choppier, and more indigenous "ska" sound that took the island by storm in the early 1960s.

There was no looking back. Helped financially by the popularity of the new music in the UK, where recordings such a Millie Small's *My Boy Lollipop* (1964) reached the upper echelons of the pop charts, ska releases flooded out of Jamaica in the mid-sixties as solo artists and groups, including the Skatalites and a threesome called the Wailers, emerged from the west Kingston slums.

The charged excitement of the ska-era dancehalls found expression in the hard-edged "rude boy" culture of sharply dressed ghetto youths who lived life on the edge of criminality – and found their lifestyle both celebrated and cautioned against in the music they danced to. As the new music progressed in the mid- to late-1960s, the musicians, weary of its fierce pace, began to slow down the staccato-like downbeat to a more relaxed and sophisticated style that became known as "rock steady."

By 1970, under the growing influence of Rasta and ganja, rock steady had slowed down even further to a chugging beat with more emphasis on a heavy bass and increasingly militant lyrics that reflected Rasta reasoning. It had become full-blown roots reggae.

In many ways, the period from the mid-1970s to the mid-1980s was the golden era of reggae, both commercially and creatively. The newly conscious lyrics, with their focus on peace and love, Garveyism, Rastafarianism, and the suffering of ghetto youths, struck a chord with audiences around the world. Many artists were able to sign big deals with international record companies and tour Europe and North America for weeks on end. A series of legendary figures emerged, including the likes of Dennis Brown, Gregory Isaacs, Jimmy Cliff, Burning Spear, and Bob Marley.

Robert Nesta Marley was a musical genius who took reggae to its greatest heights and, in the process, became the most famous Jamaican of all time. Born in 1945 to a white father and a black mother in the remote north central village of Nine Miles, his family circumstances led him as a 12-year-old to the slums of Trench Town, where he survived as best he could. A talented singer and guitarist, he formed a singing trio called the Wailers

Bob Marley's birthplace, Nine Miles

David Constantine/Panos Pictures

Bob Marley's "Inspiration stone", Nine Miles
David Constantine/Panos Pictures

Devon House

Neil Cooper/Panos Pictures

Ackees for sale, Mandeville market

Marc French/Panos Pictures

Playing draughts with bottle tops

Ian Cumming

Rafting down the Rio Grande

Ian Cumming

Carnival

Ian Cumming

The doctor bird, the national bird of Jamaica

Ian Cumming

Navy Island, near Port Antoni

Ian Cumming

in 1961 with his childhood friend Bunny Livingston (who was also from Nine Miles) and a fiery new acquaintance called Peter Tosh.

The Wailers made a more or less immediate impact on the ska scene with rude boy anthems such as *Simmer Down* (1963), but despite prodigious output throughout the 1960s and a position in the vanguard of the burgeoning musical community of Rastas, they found neither fortune within Jamaica nor fame without.

In 1973 they were signed to the Island record label by the white Jamaican entrepreneur Chris Blackwell. The deal was to prove a turning point, not just because Tosh and Livingston's distrust of Blackwell led to a split one year later, but because Island's marketing strategy quickly brought Marley's music to the attention of the rest of the world. With a new Wailers band behind him, plus the I Threes back-up singers (who included his wife Rita Anderson), he embarked on an ambitious touring schedule to support a series of classic albums such as *Rastaman Vibration, Survival*, and *Exodus*.

Marley's musical message, allied to his charisma and intense aura of spirituality, made him an international star as well as a hero in his homeland. Always keen to talk and sing about social issues, he was perceived in some quarters back home as a PNP supporter, and in 1976 narrowly escaped death during an assassination attempt at his home in Hope Road, Kingston. Two years of self-imposed exile followed, but he returned in 1978 to re-affirm his almost mythical status by bringing together Edward Seaga and Michael Manley at the outdoor One Love Concert, to the awesome accompaniment of real-life bolts of lightning. In similarly dramatic and emotional circumstances, he sang his majority rule anthem, *Zimbabwe*, at the crowning moment of that country's long-awaited independence celebrations in 1980.

The same year, however, Marley discovered he had cancer. On May 21, 1981, despite extensive treatment in Europe and the US, he died at the age of 36.

The grief in Jamaica was unbounded. After a state funeral service under the auspices of the Ethiopian Orthodox Church in Kingston, his coffin was driven along the long, winding road to his birthplace in Nine Miles. An estimated half of the island's entire population lined the route or crowded the hills around the tiny village, where he was laid to rest in a small mausoleum.

Marley's death was a huge blow to Jamaican music, but reggae had become a strong enough force to progress without him. While the Wailers had been following a melodious path during the 1970s, reggae had also been celebrating the emergence of the more dissonant "toasting" style of DJs such as I Roy, Big Youth, and later Yellowman, who sang and rapped

Wining down at the Carnival

Ian Cumming

over pre-recorded backing tracks ("dub plates") in the dancehalls. With new studio techniques being cooked up all the time, "dub" also became an art form in itself, as engineers and producers such as King Tubby added echo, reverb, and various sounds to instrumental backing tracks.

By the mid-1980s, however, a radical change was on the way. A little known DJ called Wayne Smith, in league with the producer Prince Jammy, transformed the scene with a futuristic new rhythm cobbled together on a Casio keyboard for his 1985 song *Under Me Sleng Teng*. The "digital" sound took Jamaica by storm, spawning hundreds of imitations.

The new stripped down sound, which became known as "ragga" from the ragamuffin, rude boy style culture that surrounded it, quickly drew reggae away from Rasta-inspired lyrics and melodies. Many aficionados – particularly from abroad – disapproved of the barely recognizable new sound and the "slackness" of the gravel-voiced new DJs, who largely concentrated on gun talk or sexual innuendo rather than political and social comment. But the dancehall patrons loved it.

Although the commercial initiative and much of the foreign audience gained by Marley was lost in the late 1980s and early 1990s, ragga artists such as Shaggy, Beenie Man, and Shabba Ranks were huge hits in the UK and the US, and the new style and fashion that surrounded ragga had a big influence on many musicians, especially those in the hip hop arena.

Since the digital era, some reggae rhythms have, if anything, became even more sparse. But many of the singers who emerged from ragga – most notably Buju Banton – have put their style and outlook onto a more spiritual plane, while some more traditional singers, such as Luciano and Everton Blender, have been able to come to the fore. An impressive new generation of DJs, including Sizzla and Capleton, are as militant, original, and Rasta-orientated as anything that has gone before, while slackness, though still a dancehall draw, is much less in vogue.

Although live music is a feature of life in Kingston, and Jamaica's annual Reggae Sunsplash event is a world-renowned showcase for the art form, it is in the dancehall that most Jamaicans still gain access to their music. There is little to match the excitement generated by a top sound system such as Stone Love in full flow, as the selector (who carefully picks the records to suit and cultivate the mood) and the DJ (who plays them and often raps over the top) work the crowd with specially recorded sound effects and carefully interspersed pre-releases of new material.

While posses of outrageously dressed "dancehall queens" gyrate and "wine down" to bass speakers that shake the foundations, their male counterparts strut and pose menacingly as security guards and police with guns patrol the outside. Dancehalls have never been places for the fainthearted.

Throughout the move from R&B to ska, to rock steady, roots reggae, and ragga, the sound system culture has remained the key to Jamaican music's vitality and rebelliousness, the natural focal point for the poor Jamaicans who give it its direction. Whatever path reggae has taken, it has nearly always looked to the dancehall for its inspiration.

Art and Literature

The orally-based and largely African-influenced artistic traditions of Jamaica's black majority were ignored or frowned upon by the white minority for centuries, while the whites themselves, few in number and trapped in the deadening atmosphere of plantation life, made little contribution to literature even when judged by European standards.

By the 1920s and 1930s, however, a gradual upsurge in activity from more consciously black but Western-influenced artists began to make itself felt in Jamaica, as it did in the rest of the Caribbean. Linked to the first stirrings of nationalism and the awakening of a decidedly Jamaican identity, its literature began to value the use of "dialect," its music accepted African rhythms, and its painting and sculpture adopted "primitive" or naive techniques.

Ironically, it was an English-born sculptor, Edna Manley, the wife of Norman and mother of Michael, who did much to nurture this new movement. A much-admired artist whose sculptures can be still seen around the island, she is widely considered the mother of contemporary art in Jamaica, and was instrumental in establishing the Jamaica School of Art and the National Gallery of Jamaica, which houses an impressive collection of Jamaican art from the 1920s onward.

The appreciation of non-European art styles that she and others helped to encourage lent some recognition to a number of poor, self-taught painters, such as Henry Daley (a plumber by trade) and John Dunkley (a barber), whose simple, striking work before the Second World War set standards for much of the primitive art that followed, from the likes of Gaston Tabois, Ras Dizzy, and Kapo Reynolds – as well as the more internationally influenced painting of Karl Parboosingh, Albert Huie, and Barrington Watson.

From the tourist craft markets to the small galleries dotted around the island, representational art has remained the dominant tradition in Jamaica, although since the 1950s there has been more interest in an abstract movement based around artists such as David Boxer, Carl Abrahams, and Colin Garland. Much of Jamaican art continues to explore themes of racial identity.

In literature, Claude McKay emerged in the 1920s as one of the first black Jamaican writers to be taken seriously, although he made his name mainly in the US with best-selling works, such as *Home to Harlem* and *Banjo*, which deal with the suffering of poor black Americans.

In the 1940s a group of writers collected around Jamaica's first literary magazine, *Focus*, which was launched in 1943 and edited by Edna Manley. Vic Reid became the first of the writers to be published with a historical novel, *New Day* (1949), which broke new ground by dabbling in Creole language and dealing with the inequalities of colonialism. Another member of the Focus group, Roger Mais, pushed things further with two uncompromising and controversial novels – *The Hills Were Joyful Together* (1953) and *Brother Man* (1954) – about ghetto life and Rastafarianism in Kingston, which he had experienced first hand after moving to the city as a young man from the rural parish of St. Thomas.

Others outside the group began to take up the mantle, with Orlando Patterson echoing the Kingston slum themes of Mais in his highly acclaimed novel *The Children of Sisyphus* (1964), and Louise Bennett attaining universal popularity with her down-to-earth poems and stories in pure Jamaican Creole. Known affectionately as "Miss Lou," she also made her name as a larger-than-life singer and actress, appearing in many pantomimes and becoming a renowned storyteller of Anancy-style folktales

73

(collected in *Anancy and Miss Lou*). Despite some initial snobbery, she has come to be accepted as one of the island's treasures.

The use of Creole language is now an accepted feature of most Jamaican literature and has been used to great effect by a generation of authors, including the Rasta poet Bongo Jerry and Michael Smith, a talented writer of verse who at age 29 died as a result of political violence.

More recently Erna Brodber, whose complicated, almost hallucinatory first novel *Jane and Louisa Will Soon Come Home* (1980) took indigenous writing on to a new plane, has featured as one of an increasing number of Jamaican women (such as the poets Lorna Goodison and Olive Senior) whose work has been given wider recognition.

The diaspora has provided a significant readership for Jamaican literature, but has also been a source of literary talent in its own right, beginning with Andrew Salkey, who was educated in Jamaica but moved to England and wrote two novels *A Quality of Violence* (1959) and *Escape to an Autumn Pavement* (1960), which dealt with the West Indian experience in post-war Britain. The Jamaican-born poet Linton Kwesi Johnson, who moved to Britain at the age of eleven, achieved fame in the 1970s by tackling racism and police harassment in the classic *Dread Beat and Blood* (1976). By putting many of his poems to reggae music he also helped forge a "Dub Poet" tradition that includes Mutabaruka and Jean Binta Breeze, whose debut *Riddym Ravings* was published in 1988.

Theater and Cinema

An identifiably Jamaican theatrical movement only emerged in the 1940s, but has been in good shape ever since and is one of the healthiest in the Caribbean, fortified by well-respected local playwrights such as Carey Robinson, Sam Hillary, Barry Reckord, Evan Jones and Trevor Rhone. One of its most popular mainstays is the pantomime season, which usually runs from Boxing Day to April. Pantomime, with its low-brow and loose framework of European folk tales such as *Cinderella* and *Puss in Boots*, is a perfect outlet for Jamaica's ribald strain of humor, as well as the melodramatic comic talents of actors such as Oliver Samuels. It also panders to the nation's general love for storytelling, song and dance and crowd participation. Jamaican audiences like to be part of the action rather than mere spectators, and will shout and interject from the stalls whenever possible.

The Little Theatre Movement, founded in 1941, is one of pantomime's main exponents. The oldest theatrical company in the Caribbean, it has its own "Little Theatre" in Kingston, which also houses the internationally acclaimed National Dance Theatre Company of Jamaica. But there are always long runs of rival pantomimes across the city at the elegant Ward Theatre, whose current building dates from 1911.

While pantomime and the emergence of Jamaican playwrights has made the theater more accessible for many ordinary Jamaicans, cheap cinema has long been one of their main sources of entertainment and escapism. Films have had a significant influence on popular culture, right from the days when westerns, war films, and gangster movies fed into sixties rude boy culture. From the Skatalites' *Guns of Navarone* onward, film references and titles have provided a rich source of material for successive generations of musicians and DJs.

Jamaica has also had one cinematic triumph of its own: the highly successful and critically acclaimed low-budget feature film *The Harder They Come* (1972). Starring reggae singer Jimmy Cliff, it followed the rise and fall of Rhygin, a poor country boy who comes to Kingston to make an honest living as a singer but finds himself drawn into gangsterism. In a reversal of the usual format, it was turned into a well-received novel by Jamaican author Michael Thelwell.

Despite the film's popularity, not much has followed in its wake apart from one or two inferior efforts such as *Countryman* in the 1980s and *Dancehall Queen* a decade later. Jamaica may have the talent and the subject matter to make good films, but it simply does not have the money.

Sport

As in music, Jamaica has maintained a disproportionately high profile in sport over the past 50 years, holding its own with some of the world's top sporting nations despite having little sporting infrastructure. It has significant achievements to its name in boxing, cricket, cycling, athletics, weightlifting, and more recently, in soccer. Bizarrely, it has even managed to produce a bob-sled team that achieved worldwide fame by competing in the Winter Olympics and provided raw material for the successful Walt Disney film *Cool Runnings*. Women's sport has been especially successful, boasting one of the top netball teams in the world (consistently in the top five) and a field hockey team that has been as high as third in the world rankings.

In track events, Jamaicans have won numerous Olympic and world championship medals, particularly over the sprint distances. Arthur Wint set the standard by winning a gold in the 400m in 1948, the first time Jamaica had competed in the Olympic Games. Don Quarrie then won Olympic silver medals in the 200m and 100m in 1976, Grace Jackson took silver in the 200m in 1988, Juliet Cuthbert likewise in 1992, and Deon Hemmings won a gold in the 1996 400m hurdles. In Merlene Ottey,

Jamaica has also had one of the most popular and successful sprinters of all time, although she has famously never managed to win a gold in the Olympics.

Ottey, like many Jamaican athletes, managed to rescue herself from poverty by coming through the well-organized school athletics system, which is built around the annual boys and girls "Champs" competitions. A major televised sporting event on the island, the boys and girls competition pits schools against each other at the National Stadium, with the pick of the young athletes often moving on to compete in the US or take up college scholarships.

More than 30 Jamaican schools habitually take part in the prestigious three-day Penn Relays in Pennsylvania, with the best of them snagging many of the prizes. School rivalries are intense, and although facilities are often basic it is not unusual for pupils to be instructed by former international runners. Success has brought success, with hordes of children eager to taste the kudos and financial rewards that can come with wearing the Jamaican vest.

Cricket

In a country where cricket comes close to being a national obsession, January 29, 1998 proved to be a day of disgrace for Jamaica. On that sensational Thursday an eagerly awaited five-day game between England and the West Indies at the imposing Sabina Park ground in Kingston became the first international cricket match ever to be abandoned due to an unfit pitch. Play lasted for only 56 minutes, during which time the England physiotherapist came onto the field six times to treat England batsmen injured by balls flying off the uneven grass surface.

The Sabina Park debacle was front page news for days in the English-speaking Caribbean, as commentators and politicians agonized over the fact that the island could no longer even organize a cricket match with any success. To many, the sad affair summed up Jamaica's long-term malaise.

Despite the disappointments of that day – and increasing competition from basketball and soccer – cricket is still the unchallenged national game of Jamaica. When the West Indies play international "test matches" at home, all other programming on the island is blocked out, as both main TV channels show the match simultaneously. Radio stations broadcast ball-by-ball commentary from 10am to 5pm.

Jamaica's national side has had plenty of success in the regional one-day and four-day competitions against Barbados, Trinidad & Tobago, Guyana, the Windward Islands, and the Leeward Islands, and is arguably the third most prominent cricketing nation in the Caribbean after Barbados and Guyana. A number of its players are regularly selected to play for the West Indies side, which completely dominated world cricket from the mid-1970s to the mid-1990s before returning to more mortal status among the major cricket-playing nations of Australia, England, Pakistan, and India.

Although cricket was introduced into Jamaica by the British in the second half of the nineteenth century, it was virtually restricted to whites until the beginning of the 1900s, when the black population fought to create a bridgehead into the top echelons of the game. By the 1930s, the immensely talented black Jamaican batsman George Headley made the case for equality by becoming one of the acknowledged all-time greats of the sport. His well-supported campaign to become the first black captain of the West Indies, though never conceded by the white cricketing authorities, became intertwined with the black consciousness and independence movements of the era, and helped turn cricket into a political and cultural arena of great importance in Jamaica.

It also opened up the field to new Jamaican talents such as the influential 1950s spin bowler Alf Valentine, and began the process by which black cricketers started to reinvent the English game as an exciting, flamboyant art built around fast bowling and aggressive batting. Jamaicans have played a significant role in that process, not least as members of the all-conquering West Indies sides of the 1970s, 1980s and 1990s, when the batsman Lawrence Rowe, the wicketkeeper-batsman Jeffrey Dujon and the fast bowler Michael Holding (perhaps the most gracefully lethal "quickie" of all time) came to epitomize all that was great about the regional game. They were followed by another top Jamaican fast bowler, Courtney Walsh, who captained the West Indies.

While the most talented players usually have to go abroad to earn money, cricket in Jamaica is played to a high standard at club level during a season that runs from January to the end of May. Below that, ordinary enthusiasts stage impromptu matches on any handy patch of worn grass, shantytown street or stretch of beach. Men and women follow the game with more or less equal enthusiasm.

Apart from cricket, British rule has also left an enduring Jamaican enthusiasm for horse racing. Betting shops all over the island are crowded with punters trying their luck on UK races as well as twice-weekly meetings at the sanded Caymanas Park track just outside Kingston. Golf remains too, but is hardly a mass participation sport. There are eleven courses on the island, played almost exclusively by tourists and the rich elite.

Celebrations at the
World Cup qualifier   *Ben Radford/Allsport*

The Reggae Boyz

Jamaica was a footballing backwater until the mid-1990s. Then, out of the blue, the "Reggae Boyz" burst onto the world soccer scene with unprecedented force. Much of the credit for the transformation in the national team's fortunes has gone to Rene Simoes, the deeply religious, slightly eccentric Brazilian coach who brought the footballing gospel of his native land to Jamaica's exuberant young soccer talent. By encouraging the players to show off their skills and express themselves, Simoes produced a team that not only achieved good results, but did so with style. He also made judicious use of up to half a dozen British-born professionals of Jamaican extraction whose experience in the English Premier League lent steel to the trickery.

With a galvanized public behind the team, Jamaica became the first English-speaking Caribbean nation to qualify for the World Cup finals, clinching its place in November 1997 with a tense 0-0 home draw against Mexico that led PJ Patterson to declare a spontaneous (and technically illegal) public holiday of celebration.

For a time the fortunes of the team in yellow and green eclipsed all other sporting interest on the island as Jamaicans basked in the global exposure of the forthcoming finals in France and an increasingly long unbeaten home run on the controversially bumpy pitch of the National Stadium. The colorful and well-marketed Reggae Boyz identity also caught the imagination of the rest of the soccer world – and assured enthusiastic support from millions of neutrals.

No-one expected the Reggae Boyz to go far in the finals – and they didn't – but the Jamaicans acquitted themselves well in their three games before going out at the first stage. Their one victory, a 2-1 defeat of Japan, assured a tumultuous welcome home.

Since the World Cup, however, the fortunes of the Reggae Boyz have taken a distinct turn for the worse, both on the field, where they have suffered heavy losses, and off the field, where financial problems have reared their head despite the millions of dollars that poured in from the adventures in France.

Amid whispers of corruption, the Jamaica Football Federation has had to severely curtail its funding of youth soccer, thereby increasing the likelihood that the nation will fail to capitalize on the immense grassroots interest generated by the national team's success. While some of the World Cup stars have gone abroad, the semi-professional national premier league from which they emerged at clubs like Wadadah, Boys Town, Tivoli, and Reno struggles with poor finances and even poorer facilities.

Social disparities have also reared their ugly head. Ordinary Jamaicans once gained entry to home games relatively cheaply, but with the success of recent years they have been priced out of the National Stadium, with a resultant drop in attendances, atmosphere, and general enthusiasm. As is often the case in Jamaica, something of great promise appears to have been brought low by greed and bad management.

Food

Jamaica's food has a rich cultural identity all of its own. While eating out in restaurants is generally the preserve of tourists or the elite, the island has developed a home cooking tradition as distinctive as any on the globe.

The strangely textured yellow fruit of the ackee tree, for instance, is hardly eaten anywhere else in the world, yet in the form of ackee and saltfish is the national dish of the island. Ackees, which are poisonous until the outer casing of the fruit has opened, were brought from West Africa in 1778 by a slave ship captain, while salted cod was originally imported from Newfoundland to satisfy the tastes of the planters.

Breakfast is a big meal in Jamaica, often featuring not just ackee and saltfish but cornmeal porridge, bammy (a round cake of pounded cassava that is usually fried), and the spinach-like callaloo, which is sold in bunches by street vendors all around the island.

Highly seasoned escovitch fish, served with peppers and onions, or "rundown" (fish boiled down in coconut milk) are the other much-favored fish dishes, but chicken reigns supreme as the main meal in most households, generally served with plantain and the omnipresent rice and peas, made either with gungo peas or red beans. The Indians have left their mark on food culture with the introduction of curry, usually in the form of curried goat.

As a rule, Jamaicans love to eat their main courses with an array of filling foods such as dumplings, festival (sweet and crusty fingers of fried flour), green bananas, yam, roast breadfruit, and a rather dry version of macaroni cheese. Desserts and pastries, too, are often on the heavy side. There is a widespread penchant for bread pudding, as well as *gizzarda*, made from shredded coconut and nutmeg, and sweet plantain tarts.

Favorite snacks are meat patties (developed from Cornish pasties) or "bun and cheese," which usually features processed cheese in two slices of dark malt loaf bread. But the uncontested street food of Jamaica is jerked meat, a style of cooking that is thought to have been developed by the Maroons. Every evening the smoky smell of jerk pork or jerk chicken pervades the air as street-side chefs barbecue various meats in a spicy jerk sauce for night owls returning from rum shops or dancehalls.

Although Jamaican food is essentially healthy, its high calorific values, allied to a growing fondness for the junk food now available in most town centers, means that obesity is a growing phenomenon. A slim figure, however, is not as prized in Jamaica as elsewhere in the world. Many men covet women with ample figures and "big body gals" are often praised in song. In fact there were problems during the 1980s with women taking pills designed to make them put on weight.

WHERE TO GO, WHAT TO SEE

Most visitors to Jamaica inevitably head for the world-renowned beaches of the north coast, where most of the hotels and facilities have been built over the past 30 years.

Although the coastline from Ocho Rios westwards to Negril is now heavily populated with hotels and condominiums, it has generally managed to escape the worst excesses of tourist development. This is partly due to government controls and planning regulations: no building in Negril, for instance, can be taller than the highest coconut tree.

Negril is the youngest and brashest of the beach areas, with much of its extensive white sands peppered with huts selling food and drink or playing music. But Montego Bay is the central focus of the tourist trade: a bright, bustling town with craft markets, well-appointed shops, its own beach, an offshore marine park with protected fish and coral reefs, and probably the best selection of restaurants of any settlement on the island. In the town center is a statue to the memory of national hero Sam Sharpe.

"Mo Bay" as the Jamaicans call it, is a good base to sign up for tours into cockpit country and Maroon villages such as Accompong (where there is an annual festival on January 6th to celebrate the Maroon treaty with the British). It is also close to a number of visitable "great houses" that were once the focus of large sugar estates – notably Rose Hall, once inhabited by the legendary and allegedly murderous white mistress Annie Palmer who was immortalized in Herbert de Lissier's 1929 book *The White Witch of Rosehall.*

Eastward along the coast from Mo Bay, two or three miles from the quiet town of Falmouth with its well preserved Georgian architecture, lies a lagoon at a place called Rock that is full of phosphorescent algae that light up if they are disturbed. Further still in the direction of Ocho Rios is Columbus Park, an "open air museum" on Discovery Bay, which marks the spot where Columbus first landed.

Ocho Rios is a favored stopping off point for cruise ships, partly because of its beaches, cafes, and bars, but mainly for the famous Dunns River Falls, which cascade into the sea from the verdant hills above. Climbing up the falls (for a fee) is one of the rituals of tourist Jamaica, as popular with daytripping islanders as it with foreigners. The attractions of Ocho Rios, have, however, pulled in a fair number of hustlers (irritating rather than dangerous) who hassle travelers with offers of drugs or other services.

The view from Noel Coward's window   *David Constantine/Panos Pictures*

Once you move eastward along the coast from Ocho Rios, things become noticeably sleepier. The quiet inlets and beaches around Port Antonio in particular have been much favored by rich film stars and celebrities, right back to the days of Noel Coward and Errol Flynn, who spent many weeks and months living there. As with much of the rest of the north coast, many of the best beaches in these parts are private and exclusive, often owned by hotels or restaurants. Although it is usually possible to spend a day on them for a fee, some are more or less permanently off-limits.

The south coast is slightly less well endowed with sandy areas, although Treasure Beach near Black River is a beautiful place much used by Jamaicans living in the Mandeville area, and the Hellshire beaches are favored by Kingstonians.

The main attraction of the southwest region is the swampy Black River Morass, where hired boats take visitors up the winding Black River in search of the crocodiles that bask in its waters. About fifteen miles to the east there are spectacular views out to the Caribbean from the top of Lover's Leap, a 1,500-ft cliff where two young slaves are said to have leapt to their death rather than face separation. Near Maggotty, the Appleton estate distillery offers tours on weekdays.

In the east, the awesome Blue Mountains are the dominant feature, as well as a destination of growing importance for eco-tourism. There are many hiking trails in the area, most of them starting from lodges built on the precipitous slopes around settlements such as Mavis Bank and Hagley

Racing at Caymans Park

Ian Cumming

Gap. One of the most popular treks is to start out from the foothills before midnight with the aim of reaching Blue Mountain Peak – the highest point on the island – in time to see the sun rise. The peak, when not shrouded in mist, has wonderful views to the southwest over Kingston and sometimes, so the guides say, as far as Cuba.

To the "back" of the mountains, on the lush Portland side, rafting on the Rio Grande opens up one of the easier ways of seeing the isolated rainforest that covers large parts of the John Crow peaks. But the hills are also home to many fascinating villages and hamlets, including the strange military settlement of Newcastle, built by the British in 1841 to avoid the yellow fever associated with lower lying ground near Kingston. Perched precariously at 4,000 ft, its main road, rather confusingly, runs into a parade ground that is still used daily by the Jamaica Defence Force.

In the shadow of the mountains on the southeast coast lies Morant Bay, an unremarkable town with a lively weekend market where Edna Manley's town center sculpture of Paul Bogle remembers the momentous events of the Morant Bay rebellion of 1865. Another monument to Bogle lies six miles away, near his home village of Stony Gut, where there are annual celebrations on Paul Bogle Day, October 11th.

Although many travelers now fly direct to Montego Bay and ignore Kingston altogether, the capital is worth a visit. Most of its old buildings have been destroyed by earthquake or neglect, and large parts of the city are ugly, dangerous and ramshackle, but it would be unwise to visit Jamaica without seeing the place that is its nerve center. Despite its fearsome reputation, Kingston (by virtue of the fact that it's off the beaten tourist track) is actually more hassle-free for travelers than most of the north coast haunts.

One of Kingston's best features is its everyday life, especially as manifested among the higglers and sno-cone sellers outside the shop fronts and rum bars of the downtown area – or in the enormous Coronation Market, where a sprawling mass of people sells every kind of fruit and vegetable imaginable. The capital is the best place to see Jamaicans at work and at play – in the side streets, on the buses, in the dancehalls and music venues where reggae rules the roost, or simply watching sport in their own idiosyncratic way – at Sabina Park for cricket (January to May) or at Caymanas Park for horse racing (all year round).

The capital does have plenty of more conventional sites to visit, too. There is the impressive, two-floored national gallery that lies not far from the harbor front and the elegant Devon House, a restored mansion that was built in 1881 by the country's first black millionaire, George Steibel. A popular place for better-off Kingstonians to buy an ice cream or sit in one of the attached coffee houses, it is an oasis of calm just down from the busy junction of Half Way Tree.

On the same street – Hope Road – lies the latter-day home of Bob Marley, now owned by his wife Rita and tastefully preserved as a museum in his memory. With some rooms kept exactly as they were and others filled with mementos and bric-a-brac, it manages to convey a relaxed, respectful view of the man – in contrast to the rather exploitative feel of the village site where Marley is now buried. Also open to the public, the mausoleum in Nine Miles is a must for Marley lovers, but has been slightly devalued by obligatory and over-priced guides who over-embellish the legend.

Kingston's other main attraction is not strictly in Kingston, but across the harbor in Port Royal, which can be reached by a half-hour ferry journey. The former wickedest city in the world is now a fishing community based around the remains of Fort Charles, which was built by the British in 1692. There is a wide expanse of beach and an old naval graveyard to the back of the settlement and access – via local speedboats for hire – to a number of uninhabited offshore cays with quiet beaches.

In Kingston, as in many areas, local buses can be a cheap and enjoyable way to travel around, but given the poor standard of many services, car hire is an option worth considering – especially as Jamaican roads are lined with stalls selling a cornucopia of goods from peppered shrimp and roast yam to coconut water, bananas, jerk chicken, honey, and mangoes. Be warned, however: Jamaican drivers are often reckless in the extreme and show little regard for their own safety, let alone anyone else's. If you're a nervous driver, it's best to find other ways of getting around.

TIPS FOR TRAVELERS

Safety

Despite the high crime rates, Jamaica is a reasonably safe place for visitors. The north coast resorts in particular are generally OK to walk around at night, although normal precautions and common sense are advisable. Most villages and small towns are sleepy and friendly.

Kingston is a different matter. Large parts of the city are given a wide berth by ordinary Jamaicans, let alone tourists, so it's unwise to start wandering into ghetto areas just to find out whether they're as bad as they're painted. The best advice is to stick to the main thoroughfares, keep your wits about you, and be careful about where you go at night.

The biggest danger in Kingston is likely to be robbery, so keep only small amounts of cash on you and don't go flashing around expensive jewelry and camera equipment. Otherwise, travelers are highly unlikely to get involved in anything serious. Most of the heavy-duty crime in the capital involves "bad bwoys" in the ghettos and will not impinge on your activities.

Gay travelers may find it easier to keep their orientation under wraps, for there is little tolerance of homosexuality anywhere on the island and some chance that outward displays of affection between men could trigger violence.

Health

There are few health problems to be wary of as a traveler. Although there are occasional outbreaks of the mosquito-born dengue fever, most serious diseases have been eradicated, and no vaccinations are required before you travel to Jamaica. AIDS and sexually transmitted diseases are the biggest worry, so safe sex is a must. Drinking water is safe throughout the island, as is food – except perhaps from the most unhygienic looking roadside stalls. Doctors and hospitals are overstretched, so medical insurance is worth having in case of emergencies.

Women travelers

As in much of the Caribbean, men in Jamaica delight in passing comments and issuing catcalls as women walk by. Local women will often shrug off the suggestions or return them with interest (to the amusement of all involved), but for foreigners unfamiliar with the badinage they may prove unnerving. Though rarely aggressive, Jamaican men can be extremely direct and have no hesitation in sizing up a woman as she walks by.

On the north coast, where some locals make a living out of liaisons with female tourists, women on their own may be assumed to be looking for a holiday "romance" and can expect to be propositioned with regularity.

Harassment is also reported on the crowded Kingston buses, where men often use the press of bodies as an excuse to rub up against women. Some parents refuse to allow their school age girls to travel on buses for this reason.

Although rape levels are high in Jamaica and domestic violence is endemic, violence against female travelers is rare.

Money

Foreign currency can be changed at any local banks, exchange bureaux or hotels; sterling or dollar travelers checks are best. Banks tend to open 9am to 4pm on weekdays but are closed on Saturdays; be prepared for lines. You are unlikely to be approached by unofficial moneychangers, but if you are, don't be tempted.

Souvenirs

The craft markets and small art galleries of Montego Bay, Ocho Rios, and Kingston offer a wide range of home-made souvenirs, particularly African-style wood carvings but also straw hats, leather sandals, bangles, and primitive paintings. Haggling is usually expected.

Duty-free shops in the shopping malls specialize more in watches, perfume, and designer jewelry, while the Bob Marley museum in Kingston sells its own brand of trinkets and clothing.

Blue Mountain coffee is worth searching out at local supermarkets because it's much cheaper locally than for export. Much the same goes for the various brands of local rum, including coconut rum, which is difficult to get off the island.

Children

Travelers with children are welcome throughout Jamaica. Single women travelling with children often report a particularly favorable response.

Drugs

Although Jamaica is synonymous in many people's minds with marijuana, the majority of Jamaicans are anti-ganja and the authorities are tough on drug dealing and possession. Ganja is widely available (and usually in stronger forms than many foreigners will be used to) but travelers caught in possession will be charged and imprisoned. Cocaine and crack are also prevalent, especially in Kingston and Negril; once again the penalties for use are severe.

ADDRESSES AND CONTACTS

Jamaica Tourist Board
801 Second Avenue
20th Floor
New York NY 10017
Tel: 212 856 9727
www.jamaicatravel.com

Jamaica Tourist Board
1-2 Prince Consort Road
London SW7 2BZ
Tel: 0207 224 0505

Jamaica Tourist Board
1 Eglinton Avenue East
Suite 616
Toronto M4P 3A1
416 482 7850

Jamaican High Commission
1-2 Prince Consort Road
London SW7 2BZ
Tel: 0207 823 9911

Embassy of Jamaica
1520 New Hampshire Avenue North West
Washington DC 20036
Tel: 202 452 0660

Jamaican High Commission
Standard Life Building
275 Slater Street
Suite 800
Ottawa KIP 5H9
Tel: 6113 233 9311

British High Commission
26 Trafalgar Road
Kingston 5
Tel: (809) 926 9050

US Embassy
Mutual Life Centre
2 Oxford Road
Kingston 5
Tel: (809) 929 4850

"For all that's Jamaican on the WWW"
www.jamaicans.com

Jamaica Today
www.jatoday.com.jm

FURTHER READING AND BOOKSTORES

Non-fiction

Barrow, S. *Rough Guide to Reggae*, London, 1997
Beckford, G. *Small Garden, Bitter Weed: Struggle and Change in Jamaica*, London, 1982
Black, C. *History of Jamaica*, London, 1983
Boot, A. *Bob Marley: Songs of Freedom*, London, 1995
Clarke, J. *Marcus Garvey and the Vision of Africa*, New York, 1974
David, S. *Bob Marley: The Definitive Biography of Reggae's Greatest Star*, London, 1983
Ferguson, J. *A Traveller's History of the Caribbean*, New York, 1999
Manley, M. *A History of West Indies Cricket*, London, 1995
Manley, M. *Struggle in the Periphery*, London, 1982
O'Brien Chang, K. *Reggae Roots*, Kingston, 1998
Owens, J. *Dread: The Rastafarians of Jamaica*, Kingston, 1976
Payne, A. *Politics in Jamaica*, London, 1988
Nettleford, R. *Jamaica in Independence*, Kingston, 1989
Pattullo, P. *Last Resorts: The Cost of Tourism in the Caribbean*, London, 1996
Thomas, P. *Jamaica: The Rough Guide*, London & New York, 1997
Webber, J. *Reggae Island*, Kingston, 1992

Fiction

Bennett, L. *Anancy and Miss Lou*, London, 1997
Brodber, E. *Jane and Louisa Will Soon Come Home*, London, 1980
de Lisser, H. *The White Witch of Rosehall*, London 1982
Goodison, L. *Baby Mother and the King of Swords*, London, 1990
Johnson, LKJ. *Dread Beat and Blood*, London, 1975
Mais, R. *The Hills Were Joyful Together*, London & Kingston, 1953
Thelwell, M. *The Harder They Come*, London 1980
Patterson, O. *The Children of Sisyphus*, Kingston, 1974

Bookstores

The Bookshop
15-17 Constant Spring Road
Kingston
Tel: 926 1800

The Kingston Bookshop
706 King Street
Kingston
Tel: 922 4056
(also at: Pavilion Shopping Mall, Half Way Tree, Kingston Tel: 968 4591)

University of the West Indies Bookshop
Mona Campus
Mona
Kingston

Bookland
Knutsford Boulevard
New Kingston

Sangsters Bookshop
Sovereign Shopping Mall,
Hope Road
Liguanea
Kingston

NB: There are also good bookshops in the two international airports and in some hotels

FACTS AND FIGURES

Geography

Official name: Jamaica
Situation: Jamaica lies between 17° and 18° N and 76° and 78° W. The third largest island of the Greater Antilles
Surface area: 10,991 sq km / 4,242 sq miles
Administrative divisions: Three counties (Middlesex, Surrey and Cornwall) divided into 14 parishes
Capital: Kingston (pop: 700,000)
Other important towns: Spanish Town, Montego Bay, Mandeville
Climate: Tropical, with prevailing winds from the northeast that ensure heavy rainfall on the north side of the Blue Mountains (up to 500cm / 197in a year). Temperatures over most of the island vary between 80 and 90 degrees Fahrenheit (27–32C) but can fall to 43F (6C) in the Blue Mountains. There are two rainy seasons, from May to June and from September to October, with the coolest period generally November to April.
Relief: More than half of Jamaica's surface lies more than 500m / 1,641ft above

sea level. On the eastern side the landscape is dominated by the Blue Mountains (2,292m / 7,402ft at their highest point) and the Rio Grande, which is the country's longest river; the middle and west is mainly a high limestone plateau that is most strikingly shaped by wind and rain in the hummocky cockpit country; along the north coast there are magnificent beaches; to the southwest there is the low-lying, swampy area of the Black River Morass.
Flora and Fauna: Although much of its vegetation has been introduced, Jamaica has a fascinating and beautiful plant life. About 3,000 types of flowering plants live on the island, many hundreds of which cannot be found anywhere else in the world, with 200 varieties of orchid, 60 of bromelia, and hundreds of different ferns. The national flower is the lignum vitae, a small tree with waxy leaves and light blue petals. Mangrove swamps feature all around the coast, as do many varieties of cacti in the

drier areas. There are many fruit-bearing trees such as the ackee, breadfruit tree, mango, coconut palm, and cashew tree, plus a few specimens of highly-prized mahogany and ebony in the Blue and John Crow mountains. The largest animal is the crocodile, still found along the Black River. Although the imported mongoose has done much damage to other animals, especially snakes, there are 24 types of lizard on the island (many of them in Hellshire), and 22 varieties of frog. Jamaica is well known for its spectacular hummingbird population, including the wonderful doctor bird (the national bird) with its striped double tail. Parrots can also been found in forest areas, as well as vultures. In the sea, manatees can be found in small numbers, as well as much bigger populations of dolphins, tuna, marlin and barracuda. Turtles and colorful reef fish are becoming rarer as many of their habitats are destroyed.

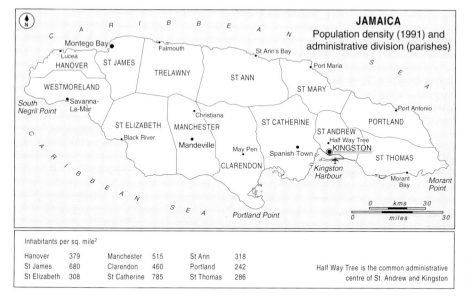

JAMAICA
Population density (1991) and administrative division (parishes)

Inhabitants per sq. mile^2

Hanover	379	Manchester	515	St Ann	318
St James	680	Clarendon	460	Portland	242
St Elizabeth	308	St Catherine	785	St Thomas	286

Half Way Tree is the common administrative centre of St. Andrew and Kingston

Population

Population: 2.6 million (1998)
Population growth rate: 1.2% (1970–90); 0.9% (1990–97)
Population density: 236 per sq km / 616 per sq miles (1998)
Urban population: 55% (1997)
Rural population: 45% (1997)
Urban growth rate: 2.3% (1970–90); 1.8% (1990–7)
Infant mortality rate: 10 per 1000 live births (1997)
Life expectancy: 75

Adult literacy rate: (1995): 85% (81% male, 89% female)
Access to safe water: 86% (1999)
Education: 96% of children complete primary school; 62% of boys and 70% of girls are enrolled for secondary school (1990–96)
Fertility rate: 2.5 (1997)
Births attended by trained health personnel: 91%
Social Development Index (UNDP Human Development Index 1999): 82nd out of 174 positions (US 3rd, UK 10th)

Religion: Baptists 18%, Anglicans 15%, Catholics 8%, Methodists 6%, Presbyterians 5%
Ethnic composition: black and mixed race 91%, whites 4%, Indians 3.5%, Chinese 1.5%
Language: English is the official language, though patois is widely spoken.
Communications: 438 radios per 1000 people (1995), 162 TV sets per 1000 people (1995); newspapers include *Daily Gleaner, The Star, Jamaica Observer, The Herald.* TV stations JBC and CVM.

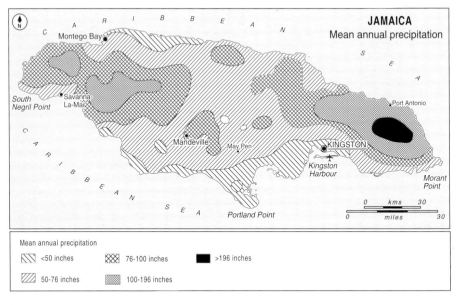

JAMAICA
Mean annual precipitation

Mean annual precipitation

▨ <50 inches	▩ 76-100 inches	■ >196 inches
▨ 50-76 inches	▨ 100-196 inches	

History and politics

Some key dates: c.650 AD: Arawaks settle on Jamaica 1494: Columbus "discovers" Jamaica and lands in Dry Harbour, now Discovery Bay 1509: Juan de Esquivel becomes first Spanish Governor 1517: First African slaves arrive 1534: Spanish Town (Villa de la Vega) founded as capital 1640: Sugar introduced as trading crop 1655: Spanish surrender to English expedition led by Admiral Penn 1670: Jamaica officially becomes British after signing of Treaty of Madrid 1692: Port Royal destroyed by earthquake 1739: Peace treaty with Maroons 1805: Slave trade abolished in British colonies

1831: Sam Sharpe slave rebellion 1838: Emancipation for slaves 1865: Morant Bay rebellion 1866: Jamaica becomes a crown colony 1872: Kingston declared new capital 1907: Earthquake destroys large areas of Kingston 1938: social upheaval and rioting as political parties and trade unions are formed 1944: Under new constitution Alexander Bustamante's Jamaica Labour Party (JLP) wins first general election under universal suffrage 1955: People's National Party (PNP) under Norman Manley wins elections for first time 1957: Full internal self-rule 1958: West Indies Federation set up 1961:

Following referendum, Jamaica pulls out of federation 1962: Full independence under JLP government 1972: Michael Manley's PNP wins elections 1976: another victory for PNP 1980: Edward Seaga secures JLP election victory 1983: Jamaica supports intervention in Grenada 1984: Early elections boycotted by PNP as JLP sweeps home to win all seats 1988: Hurricane Gilbert causes massive destruction 1989: PNP wins elections with Manley still at helm 1992: Manley resigns and PJ Patterson becomes prime minister 1993: Patterson wins convincing PNP victory over